A Faith That Fulfills

A FAITH THAT FULFILLS

By JULIUS SEELYE BIXLER

GREENWOOD PRESS, PUBLISHERS
WESTPORT, CONNECTICUT

To Martha

Contents

Acknowledgments

My first word of acknowledgement should go to Dr. Edwin McNeill Poteat, then President of Colgate-Rochester Divinity School, for the invitation to deliver these Ayer lectures in the spring of 1948, and to the faculty of the School for their cordial hospitality. Part of Chapter I has been expanded to include a portion of the Garvin Lecture delivered at Lancaster, Pennsylvania, in December, 1950, and Chapter III presents in revised form the Eugene William Lyman Lecture given at Sweet Briar College, Sweet Briar, Virginia, in March, 1949. For permission to use this material again I am grateful. My appreciation goes also to the editor of the *Harvard Theological Review* for allowing me to use in Chapter II material from an article that appeared under the name "The Contribution of *Existenzphilosophie*," to the editor of *The Crozer Quarterly* for the use in Chapter IV of material from an article called "Notes on the Problem of Suffering," and to the editor of *The Acadia Bulletin* for the use of the final illustration in Chapter VI which first appeared in an article called "Three Philosophies of Life."

Mr. Joseph Coburn Smith was the one who put me in touch with the records of the Colby religious society quoted in Chapter I. My colleague Professor John Alden Clark has given me the benefit of his comments on the manuscript.

I am grateful also to Harper & Brothers for permission to quote from *Over the Sea, the Sky* by Edwin McNeill Poteat, and to Harcourt, Brace & Co. for permission to quote from *Four Quartets* by T. S. Eliot.

J. S. B.

Colby College
Waterville, Maine
April 4, 1951

A Faith That Fulfills

I. Faith of Our Fathers

IN THE famous song of Deborah, recorded in the oldest continuous passage in the Bible, we read that by the water-courses of Reuben there were great searchings of heart. The ancient phrase speaks to us in this most modern of worlds with a peculiar poignancy. Ours is again a time of spiritual probing when motives and aims are examined with troubled urgency. It is true that the men of Reuben searched their hearts because of their failure to enlist under the banner of Barak in his conflict with the hosts of Sisera. On the surface it might appear, therefore, that we should not suffer the same pangs of remorse since we as a people have just emerged from participation in the greatest struggle of history.

But if we look deeper I think we shall discover that our own heart searchings also come from the feeling that at a time when great events are in the air we as individuals are playing the part of bystanders. It is true that our situation is complex and that our distress cannot be confined within the limits of any one formula. The hunger and agony of the devastated countries is so great that for the sake of our own mental health we dare not dwell on it too long. The plight of the displaced persons is still so serious that the thought of our comparative security brings a feeling of guilt. At the same time the idea of another war terrifies us. A glimpse of its weapons leaves us appalled that the human mind should have felt obliged to spend its inventive ingenuity in so fiendish a' way. But through all our disillusioned and almost morbid reflections runs the sharp personal challenge: What should I have done? and: What can I do now?

One result is that we are ready, as never before, for religion. I think it can also be said that large numbers of people are more ready than ever for a religion that is thoughtful. Our minds as well as our hearts are on the alert. We realize that the times call for judgment as well as devotion and we ask above all else for the kind of religious affirmation which will allow mind and heart to join forces in a common cause. The mood of wonder which is supposed to lead men to ask the larger, more metaphysical questions is already with us. The sensitiveness which reveals the deeper potentialities of love has been increased by the harrowing experiences of recent years. And the practical moral demand is so insistent as to be peremptory. So we are brought to ask with almost desperate insistence: How can society be helped to find its own good? while each of us confronts his conscience with the query: What must I as a person do to be saved?

In one sense the answer to both is easy: Love the Lord thy God and thy neighbor as thyself. But the human mind is such a strange mixture of conflicting impulses, fleeting impressions, half-formed ideas, and vacillating beliefs that it does not always understand these words or have the strength to follow them. We have also discovered that even when our motives are pure it is hard to make them fit the crosscurrents of need in a society as complicated as our own. On this account our attitude toward the troubled inquirer should mix sympathy with its censure. The question "Who is my neighbor?" is not always idle or evasive, and to cry "O that I knew where I might find Him" does not always indicate subconscious unwillingness to serve. It is true, of course, that part of our confusion is the result of sheer moral weakness and our inability to make up our minds. But the fault is not here alone. Our predicament is many sided. Along with our morals our knowledge needs to be improved.

This is why the religion of our colleges assumes greater importance than ever before. Not that in our fathers' day it was unimportant. But there has always been some truth in the statement that religious attitudes are formed in early life through the influence of home and church and that the college cannot affect their essential quality. Today, however, we see more clearly than before how close the connection between knowledge and faith must be. Of course some types of simple piety are unqualifiedly good in their place and are happily free from the nagging doubts of skeptical inquiry. Yet we must not forget that naïve belief when accompanied by mistaken ideas can be a curse. And it will hardly be denied that today any religious faith at all raises both social and cosmic questions which need precise knowledge of fact before they can be answered. Our inability to settle some of these questions has been allowed, one fears, to discourage us too easily. It is true that we know very little. But we know more than we did and we realize that such knowledge as we have must ultimately color all our loyalties and beliefs. Knowledge, in other words, is a necessary though not a sufficient condition for the right kind of religious faith. Instead of fearing it we should be on the alert to recognize its religious possibilities and to exploit them for all they are worth.

The college is an institution set aside by our society as a place where men and women may freely gather facts and work them into as coherent as possible an interpretation of human nature and its world. For the most part it has been assumed that to do this job well is to serve religious as well as intellectual ends. The majority of our colleges were founded with a religious purpose and still profess the teaching of religion as a principal aim. Why, then, should we not turn to them in this hour of despair? Will they not show us which way salvation lies?

In our more cynical moments we feel that the answer would be laughable if it were not so tragic. Can we really believe that our colleges are turning out men and women equipped to meet this spiritual crisis? But if not, why not? Our students are alert, responsive, and more mature than ever before. Our teachers are as devoted to their task as were their forebears, as truly filled with high purpose, and for the most part much better trained. Yet too much of the time and energy of students and teachers alike goes into the solution of incidental problems raised by specialized learning, leaving untouched the great issues and the great decisions they require. From one point of view it is not hard to see why this should be so. We can teach flute playing and shipbuilding and medical skills, Socrates reminds us, but virtue is something else. Particular facts can be transferred from one mind to another, but attitudes a person gains for himself. Is this, however, the whole truth? Can we give up so quickly? Attitudes are not taught in the same way, perhaps, but should we say that the teacher has no responsibility for them? The fact is that the time is too short to allow for excuses. Our colleges must formulate and teach a way of life that embodies the religion of which the world stands so sorely in need. But how shall this be done?

If anyone really had the answer he would deserve a wider hearing than even the Ayer Lectures can give him. I can at least raise the question, but I do it in the spirit of one who is eager for an answer not yet found. I should like, however, to consider with you a few of the paths our thought must travel if we are to come within hailing distance of our problem. In past years you have listened in this series to lectures on theology, archaeology, and Biblical literature by specialists in those fields. I can talk only as a humble college president (assuming the phrase is itself not a contradiction), which means as one who tries to combine the inquisitive search for ideas with the acquisitive search for gold and so to provide the means by which others can teach and learn. It is not good logic to suppose that just because one has no time for specialization he can therefore speak with authority on issues that are general. But, like virtue, education is a subject on which everyone has an opinion, and here as elsewhere we can find the truth only when each of us brings his views into the open.

I should like to start, then, with a comment on some of the changes in our religious attitudes. As we look at the records we are impressed first of all by our loss of the old-time fervor. Our ancestors lived in times that seem in retrospect less threatening than ours, yet they themselves were serious enough in their approach to the great questions of life and faith. Should they, then, be our first teachers? Or do changes in point of view make this impossible? Recently some old diaries and old minutes of religious association meetings have come to light in the Colby College archives that may help us to see what we have lost and what, if anything, we have gained. Here are a few excerpts.

On August 30, 1833, a Colby freshman wrote in his diary:

I have just entered college in order to prepare myself for the great work of preaching the gospel of Christ. I feel that the work is great, far too great for me to perform without the aid of the Holy Spirit.

The college and circumstances appear favorable to the attainment of knowledge but it is all nothing without the blessing of God. My spiritual life does but just glimmer—spirits are low, void of energy to take hold of any thing: O God remove this darkness, shine in upon my soul, make me to feel the power of thy grace; the joy of sin forgiven; for without these my course is vain and worse than in vain. I have left my friends afar but if God be glorified I am satisfied.

A few weeks later we find this entry:

I have been somewhat unwell for two or three days but retired in twilight to the banks of the Kennebec for prayer, and had a good season. I think the Lord met me. Prayed for submission to his will, if he saw fit to make me sick and take me from this world, prayed that I might acquiesce. Felt a desire for the conversion of my fellow students, some in particular in my class; but when I turned my mind to my father's family was much affected to think some of my brothers and all my sisters did not love God, consequently they were in danger of losing their souls. Tears flowed freely down my cheeks. Prayed for them. Thought what a thing it would be if I should see them not till judgment and then be separated from them.

This somewhat lugubrious note was apparently carried over into his schoolteaching, for we find this entry on December 21 of the same year. "I have finished the third week of my school. Have had about forty scholars. They appear docile. I spoke of death, judgment and eternity a few moments at the close of school. They appeared attentive—may God convert them."

Equally interesting are the records of a society of earnest Christian undergraduates who called themselves the "Pauloi" or "Pauls" in recognition of their missionary enthusiasm. The members, says the constitution, "must be whole-hearted Christians, those only who have given themselves up body and soul to the cause of our Dear Redeemer, and who earnestly desire to be engaged in the blessed work of winning souls to Christ." They resolve to read "standard religious works, e.g., Baxter's *Saint's Rest, The Reformed Pastor,* discourses of eminent preachers," and to engage in "the establishment of doctrines which we heartily believe,—not debates where one defends what he does not believe,—the bringing forward of all known arguments for, and a full consideration of everything that may be said against them." The "List of Resolves" contains two of special interest: "That I will punctually and regularly attend every college prayer meeting; as well as those of my class unless actually prevented by other and more important duties," and "that I will earnestly strive to avoid the indulgence of all foolish and vulgar jesting."

After the third meeting, October 15, 1860, "it was thought best to have the meeting at six o'clock A.M. precisely on Sabbath morning." On March 18, 1861, "It was proposed that hereafter on Monday eve the brethren omit supper and so come together for a longer time." The record continues: "One brother vigorously supported the measure claiming that literal fasting such as we read of in the Bible was a thing we knew very little about and of which it would not be an injury to know more. Was he not at least Scriptural? All the rest favored it too, and finally it was voted accordingly that on next Monday we will assemble together by fifteen minutes after prayer time and thus have a meeting less hurried and more useful."

To show that there was a lighter side I cannot resist quoting the minutes of a meeting held in November, 1860:

Everyone seemed in high spirits, and the hour was soon gone. The brethren talked of the business somewhat but without appearing to make much headway. They were rather more inclined to consider the approaching examinations, and then their probable success during the winter months' teaching.

Yet these subjects in themselves too often productive only of deep anxiety and solicitude could not hide the spirit of heartfelt joyousness which beamed in the eye and found expression in the earnest tones of the voice as our brethren talked of God's rich love shone [sic] to us during the term. They looked back to the time when we first assembled as a band of Christian brothers who had dedicated themselves wholly and without reserve to the cause of our blessed Redeemer. They thought of the increasing interest shown by the unconverted, of the displays of God's power in the conversion of souls—of the frequent seasons of refreshing which had been enjoyed at the prayer room—and of those loftier, nobler conceptions of the true Christian life which each felt that he had in some measure gained. Of these things they thought. Of these they spoke. And so the time glided swiftly away leaving—their—business—undone. It was then voted to lay the business on the table. And finally the meeting was closed with prayer.

The record for April 8, 1861, reports a "joyful" meeting—yet this was the hymn that was sung:

> Did Christ o'er sinners weep
> And shall our cheeks be dry
> Let floods of penitential tears
> Burst forth from every eye.
>
> The son of man in tears
> Angels with wonder see
> Be thou astonished oh my soul
> He shed these tears for thee.
>
> He wept that we might weep
> Each sin demands a tear
> In heaven alone no sin is found
> And there's no weeping there.

On May 27, 1861, the handwriting is different and a note is introduced with which we ourselves are too sadly familiar. "Voted to draw up a resolution in behalf of those who have gone into their country's service." The minutes continue through the spring of 1862 and the rest is silence.

What shall we say of these voices from the past with their

queer mixture of the familiar and the strange? At the outset we are struck by the fact that we have either lost entirely or else retained only in a more obscure form certain items of belief that to them were fundamental. First and most serious is our loss of a clear-cut idea of the nature of the highest good and the manner of its appearance to men. These Christians of an older day knew definitely whom they loved and how they could serve him. In this respect they were better off than we. It is hard to trust life when one knows that there is so much about it one does not know. To be unsure of the presence of one increasing purpose in the world is to have less confidence in special purposes of one's own.

Second, we have lost belief in a judging Presence. Perhaps our motives can be made more pure on that account and we can be brought to love a God of righteousness for what he is rather than for what he may do to us. But the older feeling of intimate relation to a personal Judge present in the hour of temptation is something that we fallible mortals can ill afford to leave behind.

Third, we have lost the feeling our fathers had of the nearness of the spiritual world and its responsiveness to all our higher intuitions. "Nothing is so beautiful," said Arthur Clutton Brock, "as the light in a cottage window, except the light of the stars; . . . and our desire is to be sure that the stars are the lights of home with the same spirit of home behind them." But as far back as the seventeenth century George Herbert expressed our modern mood when he said:

> O rack me not to such a vast extent
> These distances belong to thee.
> The world's too little for thy tent
> A grave too big for me.

Today our knowledge of the stars' radioactivity has not increased our feeling for their radiance, and their numbers suggest infinite mystery rather than majesty. We do not know where we belong.

Fourth, we no longer know who we are ourselves. Without even gaining the world we have lost our souls. It may be true that our glib modern talk about unconscious drives and conditioned reflexes does not leave us so spiritually empty as we are tempted at first to assume. Those who try hardest to interpret the mind as merely the body under another name seem to forget that the use of argument itself presupposes a belief in the kind of reasonableness that belongs to mind alone. But the new theories in this field have come so fast and gone so far that their apparent negations have confused us. We know there is such a thing as spirit, but we are not sure how to define it and our lack of confidence makes us slow to use its distinctive qualities. Particularly are we baffled when we try to think of the form it may be expected to assume after death.

Finally, we have lost our faith in the church partly because the church itself is confused. One says this in the mood of a confessor, not a censor. The blame is our own. If we want the church to lead we must ourselves help to point out the forward path. As Rufus Jones has put it: "The word 'church' is to many scientific-minded persons a word of offense. It ought to be a word denoting friendship, fellowship, and service."

When, however, we turn from special items of belief to changes in general attitude and temper the balance is not all on the debit side. In the first place, it is clear that the older religion was introspective to an unhealthy degree. The poor little freshman on the banks of the Kennebec weeping for his brothers and sisters who would probably be damned makes us smile, and not with envy. The concern for the unconverted classmates seems to us priggish. It is of course true, as these examples themselves show, that agony over one's own soul could in special instances lead to forgetfulness of oneself in the sacrificial service of others. But I think it is not unfair to say that often it resulted only in morbid sentimentality. Conviction of sin is not enough. We cannot expect it to produce either the aggressive interest in the facts or the wholehearted devotion to social causes that our times require.

College religion does well, it seems to me, to take account of this change in temper. Youth is naturally a time for introspection. We need never fear that our students will not pay enough attention to what is going on in the depths of their emotions. The question is simply whether they will keep their sense of proportion and what we can do to help them to keep it. At the right time and place retreat into the inner world of private feeling is a means to enrichment of experience and a source of moral strength. The trouble is that the tensions of our day encourage a type of withdrawal which leads to division of interest and to weakness. Through the study of literature and the arts the college should encourage the kind of exploration of inner depths which brings sensitive appreciation. Then through the more solid intellectual disciplines the student should be introduced to conceptions that are rational and universal. Feelings are private possessions, precious but dangerous. Ideas are held in common. They are patterns visible to the mind's eye, and to see them at all is to see them as other men do and to enter into an experience that is shared.

Because they are found in the life of reason and because these lectures are to deal with a rational faith we shall have much to say about these shared experiences later on. Here let us note in passing that faith is also concerned with the private and the incommunicable and that it has a special concern with them today. For no one will deny that our one hope of making up our present religious deficiencies is by balancing our loss in clarity and preciseness by a gain in richness of perception. The clarity, we must agree, has gone. The exact outlines of the older belief have faded and the tidiness of its argument will never be recovered. To learn more about some of the details than did our fathers seems only to mean that the vision of the whole moves continually farther into the background. Yet is it not true that our emotions are challenged even more poignantly than were theirs? The fact that increasing knowledge is accompanied by increasing mystery serves to stimulate our wonder. Why should we not recognize the added stimuli our age possesses and use them to heighten our sensitiveness? Should we not be more imaginative in our speculations and less tied to a conventional framework of thought? What of suffering, for example? It poses our deepest problems and presents the greatest obstacles to faith. Should we not free it from its entanglement in a theological preoccupation with sin and try to probe its mystery anew? And on the other hand what of art and our experience of the beautiful? Have we made sufficient attempt to rescue it from dogma and to allow it to tell us in its own way about the meaning of the universe?

To these questions we must return later. Let it suffice to say here that the idea of special revelation, on which the older religion was based, is itself a stumbling block today. It involves in contradictions even those who plead for it. Such writers as Barth and Brunner, for example, may argue in its behalf, but their arguments are made unconvincing by their own procedure. They themselves do not accept the entire Biblical tradition uncritically. When they go to the Bible they select from it what meets reasonable standards of usefulness and truth. In spite of themselves, that is to say, they yield to the influence of the contemporary climate of opinion and employ the tests all thinkers must use, whether believers in revelation or not. In the second place, the idea of a revelation at a special time and place is too closely linked with that of a chosen people to be entirely palatable today. Of course it is true that some creeds reveal more about God than others. But if they do, it is because their prophets and wise men have made better use than others of the senses and the wits God gave them. Their knowledge, in other words, is universal in that it is attainable by all who are ready for it. Its communication required no activity of a supernatural sort.

Instead of lamenting our losses, therefore, we should stress the fact of our gains. After all, we do not want subjectivity that is morbid, nor the kind of precision that is possible only when knowledge is incomplete, nor revelation that flouts the methods of rationality. If there is a God, we shall find him only by keeping our eyes open and our hearts attuned to what we believe to be his will. The right to inquire is autonomous. It may not be overruled by any higher authority. It is itself a gift from God, and if we respond to its demands we shall find out what we need to know about God as about all else.

I cannot help believing that our confusion stems from our basic inability to answer the ancient question of the difference between reason and faith. At the present time we have almost been jockeyed into the position of setting the two against each other. We lament the loss of faith. At the same time we observe the rapid advance of science. The fact that we have less faith and more knowledge leads us to think that the two must vary inversely and that the more we know the less we shall be able to believe. The results are felt not only in religion but wherever the higher loyalties are in question. Our advancing knowledge, for example, has not brought us more confidence in reason. Indeed, the tide seems to have turned just the other way. The cult of the so-called "demonic" in theology is only one sign. Others are the use of grotesque and irrational distortion in art and the retreat of modern literature into the depths of the unconscious.

When we stop to reflect on the matter we can hardly miss the point that this loss of confidence in reason is the result of a fundamental misapprehension. If faith goes when knowledge comes, whether it be faith in God or man, it is faith of the wrong kind. That knowledge can be used for good or evil is true, and that knowledge of facts and techniques must be accompanied by attitudes which are broad and humane everyone will agree. Yet these broader attitudes will be cultivated not by shunning knowledge or being suspicious of it when it comes but rather by making clear to ourselves the implications for the life of the spirit that the quest for knowledge itself entails. This, I think, is a cardinal item in the liberal's creed. As I understand the liberal, he is not merely asserting with Francis Bacon that knowledge is power but is pointing first to the negative fact that knowledge cannot be a barrier to the life of the spirit because the demand for more knowledge is itself a spiritual demand. And in a more positive way he affirms that the sanctions and standards of reason by which knowledge actually comes are indications of what the sanctions and standards of the moral and even of the religious life must be. The life of reason, in other words, should not be interpreted narrowly as consisting merely in grubbing for facts and analyzing their relations. It involves loyalties and disciplines of its own which help to make clear what the religious life itself requires.

Thus I think it is a great mistake when a recent influential book sets Christianity on one side and groups fascism, communism, and liberal rationalism together on the other as if these three were bound together by a common opposition to the religious beliefs we know and love. Indeed, one cannot help wondering if the opponents of liberalism who are so quick to put it outside the Christian pale have actually thought their position through. What some of them derisively call "the liberal's optimistic view," for example, is not an "ideology," to use the current word, like fascism and communism, nor is it a faith, like Christianity. It is, rather, a method which is both at the opposite pole from the ideologies and also a necessary supplement and adjunct to Christian belief. Primarily it is an instrument for use in attacking the problems of the intellect. It is the conviction that if we can get the facts and arrange them coherently we shall go forward in our thinking. And the liberal is not alone in this confidence. Certainly the man in the street has it, whether he goes to the right or left or down the middle of the road. If the truth must be told, the critic himself uses the same method as soon as he starts to criticize or takes his pen in hand to write.

Where religion is concerned, the claim of the liberal is simply that, in so far as faith involves us in questions where rational judgment is needed, the usual rational tests must be applied. It is hard to see how anyone can take another view. The only possible difference of opinion would seem to come over the question of what happens when feeling, as for example in art or friendship, takes us to experiences where thought is temporarily in abeyance. And, whether you accept it or not, the position of the liberal at this point is clear. It is, first, that whenever faith makes statements about matters that thought can check, thought is the final judge of correctness; and second, whenever faith leaves thought temporarily behind, it must do so in a way which ultimately presents new data for thought and amplifies instead of restricting its influence. Psychologically if not politically speaking, we live in one world. The tests for rational validity apply throughout its domains. It is true that the ideal of coherence may adapt itself in different ways to intellectual judgments, aesthetic emotions, and moral decisions. But in each case its demands are basically the same. Always it requires balance, proportion, and harmonious inclusiveness, and calls for the appropriate and the fit. We must agree that its meaning comes out most explicitly when it is put to intellectual use and its logic is applied to the relations holding among our ideas. But the more we study it the better we see that its tests in all areas are fundamentally alike. Yet should this surprise us? Would it not be disconcerting if the rules for validity were different for different types of value experience? In such a case how could our appraisals ever be secure?

Let us not seek to find flaws in the rules of reason, then, and exceptions to the way they apply, but let us rather see how they really operate. Instead of cutting our mental life up into compartments, why should we not make clear its unity? Let us demonstrate to our various specialists, for example, the larger aspects of their responsibilities as rational beings. If the cloistered scholar believes that when the pieces of the intellectual puzzle have been fitted together his job is done, let us remind him that to live as a reasonable man is to be ready to decide and to act. Or if, as happens so often today, the artist withdraws to the petty maladjustments of his private world and emerges only to paint a picture full of dyspeptic complaint, let us tell him also that until he has a message in which others are interested his work is not art and that he cannot communicate such a message unless he is willing to meet the tests of rational insight. Where our concern is with religious faith let us at least take two preliminary steps. Negatively, let us be sure that our beliefs are free from contradiction; more positively, let us strive to realize the kinship of our loyalty to God and our loyalty to truth.

The task confronting our colleges today thus takes its place as part of the larger task confronting all thoughtful people of defining the relation of reason to religious faith and explaining their final harmony. To study the records is to be convinced that the problem did not present itself to the older generation as it does to us. They did not feel a conflict. For them there was no suggestion that faith and knowledge might be at odds. It was only when science began to make statements denying certain tenets faith had held assured that difficulties began to arise.

It is our purpose to explore the problem of faith and reason by asking about the bearing on religious faith of various aspects of the life of culture. Next time, for example, we shall consider the challenge presented by a powerful movement in contemporary theology. Neo-orthodoxy, which lashes out against liberalism, hails Kierkegaard as its prophet and accepts his unbridgeable dichotomy between God's ways and man's, must be examined and its claims refuted if our argument is to prevail. The third lecture will go back to the Old Testament for evidence that a well-known type of religious experience, famous for both its insight and its power, is entirely in accord with rational religion as the term is here used. Following this we shall examine two special areas of our emotional life which have obvious bearing on religion but are sometimes thought of as belonging to its outer and irrational fringe. I refer to the experience of suffering and the experience of beauty interpreted by art. We shall see that the contribution of each to life as a whole is best understood when related to the demands of a rational faith. In the last lecture we shall use Arnold Toynbee's figure of "withdrawal and return" to illustrate the rhythm of contemplation and action in religion and reason alike. Here we shall pay particular attention to college life and so shall come back once again to the setting with which we began. Our claim throughout will be that on college campus as in the life of the reasonable man faith comes not to destroy but to fulfill.

II. A Faith That Falters

DID we dismiss our fathers' faith too quickly? Were we a bit hasty in claiming that it could not meet the tests of modern times? An important group of present-day theologians would say so. They would argue that we can accept all that science has to offer, including the science of Biblical criticism, and yet retain the older faith to all intents and purposes unchanged. This is a striking statement which takes us by surprise. Yet it is made by men who combine piety with learning and with an enviable record of active work for social reform. Obviously we should pay attention to it.

The basic ideas of "neo-supernaturalism" or "neo-orthodoxy" are familiar, and an extended summary will not be necessary. In effect it has emphasized anew those parts of Christian teaching that are associated with Paul, Augustine, and the Reformers. It stresses the authority of the Bible as the revealed Word of God, and in particular the Biblical doctrines of sin, judgment, grace, and the incarnation. In its most recent form it makes much of what it calls the "idolatry" of those who would select a finite good, such as "reason," or "progress" or "democracy," and try to make it into an "ultimate." Agreeing in general with the view we would take that religion is loyal devotion, it would sharply disagree with our idea that the object of loyalty is the Rational Good. This, it would say, is sheer humanism. God exists, these men claim, in a "dimension" different from ours, and His mercy must be evoked to rescue us not from this or the other particular sin but from the human predicament as such. In it we are caught as sinners who cannot save ourselves. The movement is especially violent in its treatment of those whom it calls "simple moralists" or "naïve liberals." In this respect it is extremely critical of the faith that underlies most college instruction. The liberal is the victim not only of sin but of the worst sin, which is pride, and the worst pride, that of the intellect. Our human thoughts are not God's thoughts, our righteousnesses are but filthy rags, and our virtues are hardly even splendid vices. Between God and us there is complete "discontinuity." The gap can be bridged by supernatural revelation alone.

These are important words to consider, for, if they are true, much of our present educational theory is false. A college sees the problems of the spirit through the lenses of reason and finds in philosophy a disclosure of what religion means. Yet for such a neo-orthodox leader as Karl Barth a philosophy of religion in any Christian sense represents an impossible attempt to combine conflicting interests. "There can be no Christian philosophy," he says, "for if it is Christian it is not philosophy, and if it is philosophy it is not Christian."

We can perhaps best understand how radical this statement is from the point of view of college teaching if we turn to the writer who today is hailed as a major prophet of neo-orthodoxy. Of late this man's opinions have attracted so much attention even outside religious circles that he has become almost a modern fad. Long before Barth, Kierkegaard said that there could be no Christian philosophy and urged men to turn their backs on the intellect and on all cultural values if they would find salvation. Yet by a queer twist of fate Kierkegaard today actually helps us to understand what culture means and how it is related to religion. Let us see how this can be so.

Kierkegaard is a prophet not only of orthodoxy but of subjectivity. In the previous lecture we saw that the retreat into the subjective inner mood is dangerous. But Kierkegaard seems not to see the danger, for one of his most frequently quoted statements is that "Subjectivity is the truth." Just what does he mean? Certainly he does not agree with the philosophical idealists that mind is the sole reality, for he inveighs vigorously against idealism, particularly that of Hegel, as an effort to merge the personal thinker in the broad philosophical idea. Nor does he intend to teach intellectual or ethical anarchy, for he clearly believes in some universal principles and tries to preach them to others. He does not say that each man is the measure of all things nor does he turn the phrase around and argue that the truth is merely subjectivity.

What he seems to mean is that the truth must be grasped by us in an inner experience of appropriation. We should avoid the temptation to exhaust reality by universalizing it, as thought does. With the pragmatists we should see that truth is not abstract but practical. Truth is what we do about the facts with which we are confronted. Whether you consider truth to be agreement of thinking with being or of being with thinking, he says in his famous *Postscript*, you must take account of the subject who has the thought. What are his possibilities? He cannot leave his inward predispositions behind and become wholly objective. He himself, an unreasonable person, cannot attain the serene objectivity of the truth to which he aspires. Even when the truth is his he does not become a reasonable being. A crazy man remains crazy no matter how many times he repeats the truth that the earth is round. A *Privatdocent* can say in the lecture room that everything is disputable and then go on to write his own system which will put an end to all disputes. Truth when it enters personal thought must become irrational. This is why the highest truth is not for reason but for life—a paradox which faith must accept. Truth, we say, is agreement with being. But if being is taken as empirical, it is only becoming, not real being. And if thinking is taken as not part of becoming but eternal, you lose the difference between being and thinking and have simply a tautology.

The solution comes, says Kierkegaard, when we see that Descartes's thinking ego is an abstraction from the real participating ego. The real ego combines being and thinking in active interest. Consider the distinction between essence and existence. In the world of logical essences all is necessary; in the world of existence things come into being not of necessity and therefore through freedom. Hegel dodged the problem of how the idea becomes concrete and therefore failed to show what freedom actually means. As a matter of fact, the idea becomes concrete through the active will. We know directly the logical essence or what a thing is; we do not know immediately that it is. Thus the knowledge process itself requires that we meet events in history or in the world of becoming with belief, and belief requires active faith, and faith in turn means an effort of the active will. Knowing means participation of an active sort.

It will repay us to go one or two steps further into Kierkegaard's ideas in order to be sure just what he is saying. Most of us in America are not able to read him in the original Danish, but the flexibility of his thought comes out in the German translations through which he first reached a wider audience. Take the word "existential," for example—a word that has been adopted by a recent literary cult. What did it signify as Kierkegaard used it?

We should observe that *Existenz* in the German translation

of Kierkegaard is not the same as our English "existence." An ordinary object in time and space has *Dasein* but it does not *existieren*. *Existenz* is not *Sein*, for this is too broad a term, covering being of all sorts. Nor is it *Leben*, for this is shared by men with animals and plants. *Existenz* is the property only of human beings and of only a limited number even here. The child does not have it, nor does the non-Christian. *Existenz* is the experience of the Christian believer as he develops his spiritual powers, faces crises, makes decisions, and summons his whole personality to meet the demands of faith. *Existenz* is *reduplication*, which means meeting the timeless idea in such a manner that it is lived over again in personal experience. Faith is private life where both ethics and reason are public and universal. This means that where ethics discusses and argues faith is silent. Ethically and for argument, Abraham's willingness to sacrifice Isaac was murder, but for faith it was loyal obedience. In its personal privacy faith takes the revelation of the Incommensurable as that which cannot be measured or reasoned or proved. The God-man, incommensurable by our standards, came into history incognito as a child in the manger, a King in the form of a servant. This is the supreme paradox which the believer must accept. To the Jews (that is, the practical reason) it is an offense, to the Greeks (that is, the pure reason) foolishness, to the Christian (that is, to faith) salvation. In the paradox religion God shocks man into obedience by revealing that what could take place only contrary to human understanding has actually become history.

So, concludes Kierkegaard, no complacent professor of philosophy need suppose that through his own philosophical acumen he can find the way to God. And so, conclude his modern expositors, to apply reason is to show to what lengths of effrontery men can be driven by the promptings of an egocentric pride.

What a challenge Kierkegaard presents to our modern approach with the coolly confident air we must confess that we are too prone to adopt! How right is the claim that the personal characteristics of life distort the abstractness of thought and how great must the distortion be when thought tries to serve as an intermediary between poor frail man and the Highest that can be known! Sometimes it seems as though we should hail Kierkegaard as one of the greatest among the prophets because of the clearness with which he sees the sin of *hybris* and the zeal with which he tries to protect us from it.

And yet, upon reflection we can only feel that he goes too far. Man does, after all, approach the Highest, and it is humility rather than pride that prompts him to believe that the Highest can be known. Further, it is the hope of communion with the Highest that keeps his own will alert. Any word, even the word of philosophy, may lose abstractness and therefore purity when it takes on flesh, but surely flesh takes on purity and reasonable form when the word enters into it. When reason controls nature, nature itself becomes reasonable. Whatever the puzzles of "being" and "becoming" and the differences of essence from existence, we cannot believe that it is always and everywhere impossible for truth about spiritual things to be learned and to prevail. Whatever our disagreement with the effort of the philosophical idealists to show that all is mind or dependent on mind for its existence, we can only applaud their conviction that when thought is in control the life that harbors it is raised to a higher than natural level. We are foolish, after all, if we allow Kierkegaard to persuade us that men cannot ever think straight or that there is any final moral or logical obstacle to straight thought about God. Of course pride does often set up a barrier. Yet there have been philosophers who were not complacent, and the presence of only one would be enough to upset Kierkegaard's sweeping generality. Indeed, if thought about God is not possible we may as well stop using the word and resign ourselves to the fact that in religion we employ terms without knowing what they mean. In some respects this is what Kierkegaard does. But instead of shrinking from this conclusion he seems to glory in it. For him it is a way of emphasizing his belief that God's communication with us is through a method wholly out of line with anything else that we know.

Now, what is this method? It is that of special supernatural revelation. But what is special revelation? From our point of view, as Kierkegaard says, it is absurd and a scandal. Why does it seem scandalous to the modern mind? If Mr. A or Saint B or Prophet C has a revelation—what really happens? Probably he uses the word "revelation" in the first place because the experience comes suddenly or with unusual force so that the circumstances surrounding it seem strange. Yet as soon as the one who has it receives it as true, fits it into his own pattern of thought, and tries to do something about it, he finds that in spite of himself he has tested it by the same rational and practical standards he uses for everything else that comes into his mental life. Where, then, is its special quality? Usually the person says of it that it comes with love, it brings him to judgment, and it requires of him moral action. But why should we call this "supernatural"? Many modern writers try to meet the difficulty by saying that revelation belongs to a moral rather than an intellectual category. For example, Barth and Brunner affirm that God reveals not divine truths but divine acts and that he does not so much offer knowledge as confront man with an issue that forces action.

But does this mean that when he calls on men to act God intends to by-pass man's own best critical judgment? It is hard to believe so. Indeed, the Biblical writers themselves knew better. Along with its commandments revelation in the

Bible brings statements of what is true. God himself not only acts; he speaks and tells men what to believe. Further, it would be impossible to command moral action without giving an intelligible clue to the nature of the action. Nor is the case made easier by the claim that revelation is necessary because sin blocks our apprehension of rational truth. That sin blocks insight is a fact but this applies to revealed as well as to rational insight. If we are to know the truth we must get rid of sin, and if we are to get rid of sin we must indeed have God's help. But the point of this whole discussion is that God works through the best that we know—our best love, our best will, our most reasonable strivings after righteousness and truth—and not through a miraculous dispensation which leaves us confused. "He who disparages reason on behalf of revelation," said Locke, "puts out the light of both."

One must charge Kierkegaard, therefore, with having failed to make clear how we can responsibly accept a revelation that offers itself on the basis of its own sovereign or special supernatural authority and boasts of its independence of our critical processes. It is not enough to dismiss this as a "paradox," on the supposition that it is easier to take under that name. What Kierkegaard must mean is that it is a seeming untruth or an insufficiently clarified truth which, when accepted and made a guide for life, will in the end justify itself as true. As a matter of fact, this is really the explanation he gives as he goes on. What is accepted in humility, he says, may approve itself to reason and work for righteousness. In emphasizing the progressive resolution of the mystery through advancing experience he actually takes the sting out of the supernaturalism he called upon at first.

If, therefore, we take the drift of his argument rather than his actual words we find that he gives us a clue to what happens in the unfolding of the religious life. We start with an innate capacity for moral achievement, for in spite of what

Kierkegaard says we should not get anywhere without it. But because this capacity is so closely linked with what is most deeply personal and individual about us we must admit that it brings an air of mystery and unclassifiability. We go on to accept a message that seems to come to us from God because, although we may not wholly understand it, we can see that it is in line with our conception of the Rational Good. As we live with it and grow into its meaning we find various ways of putting it to the test. Yet we never wholly lose our sense for its problematic nature, including the mysteriousness of the fact that we are here at all and find the promptings to the better life that we do. The real dialectic of experience is to be found in this alternation of mystery and rational criticism, but it is the critical process that sets the tone for both understanding and action and not, as Kierkegaard would have it, the mystery.

Certainly also there is a sense in which Kierkegaard is correct when he says that "Subjectivity is the truth." Much of the time we live in a common universe of discourse where communication, though incomplete, is adequate. There are, however, depths of privacy that cannot be shared. With these as "what a man does with his solitariness" religion is particularly concerned. But even here what is universal and what is individual should not be set over against each other as if they were in contradiction. As we shall see in the next lecture, when we look at the prophet Hosea, withdrawal into the depths of personal feeling may reveal the presence of that which man shares not alone with his fellows but with the great Spirit of the universe itself. Classicism has grasped the lesson that the surest way to communicate is to point to form in its rational clarity. Beethoven, for example, uses many devices, including the almost primitive resort to percussion instruments, to beat out patterns of rhythm that the mind can accept and understand. But Beethoven knows also how to make the heart respond to the sheer romantic appeal of beautiful sounds. The shared experience that romanticism brings is not so easy to point out or explain but it is there nevertheless. Our whole quarrel with the neo-orthodox thus comes down to the fact that they have made too sharp the distinction between what we have in private and what we hold in common. It is true that life presents us with a polarity which requires us at times to withdraw into our own isolated selves. But the isolation is not so complete as they would make it. It involves no "incommensurability." Nor do we have to be rescued from it by supernatural action. The rhythms of experience itself provide for the needed return. Indeed, if the break is as sharp as they say, and if the rational is as irrelevant to the religious life as they profess, one wonders why they bother to write books in which the appeal to reason is made.

We face here, that is, a situation for which "paradox" is too mild a term and which actually involves a contradiction. Certainly Kierkegaard was an unusual man with virtues that deserve our respect. But we ought to be clear that consistency was not one of them. He professed to distrust words, yet in his short life he spent a large amount of time with words and succeeded in putting an extraordinary number of them on paper. He inveighed against abstract ideas but he used them with great success. He apparently loved writing so much that he allowed it to divert time from what he would have called more Christian pursuits. He was unable, also, to meet the social requirements he himself laid down. One ought, he said, to take part in the world's work—have regular employment, establish a home, raise a family, vote and fight for social betterment. Yet he himself did none of these. He advocated social reform yet turned his back on the revolution of 1848 and said of the liberal constitutions of his time that they aroused "longing for an Eastern despotism as something more fortunate to live under." A fierce opponent of pride in others, he found it hard to conquer in himself, as shown by his almost abnormal sensitiveness when he was lampooned in the press. He preached beautiful sermons on love, yet his recorded attitude toward his contemporaries was bitter and he based his religion on anxiety.

Consider also the strange way in which he both hid behind his own writings and strutted conspicuously in front of them. For the most part he wrote under a pseudonym, as if unwilling to let his authorship be known. Yet there is hardly a book in which under extremely thin disguises he does not bare his soul's inmost life. Continuous are the references to his most private feelings, such as his shock at discovering his father's morbid depression and his agony over his own temptations. His books seem actually to exploit his unhappy love affair and broken engagement with Regine Olsen, and the more one hears of it the more glad one is for Regine that the relation terminated when it did!

Kierkegaard preached the weakness of the individual but he was sure of his own genius and counted on the applause of posterity. He taught that each must come to God in his own way yet was confident that he himself could serve as an intermediary and could show the path that others must follow. Such were the results of his retreat into his own private life and his appeal to the incommunicable. That religion encourages one kind of subjective withdrawal we have already noted. But Professor Whitehead, who has set this forth most persuasively, has also shown how sharable is the essential vision, how universally valid are the objects of sensitive experience, and how regular are the laws of communication. Plato saw, as clearly as any other, the abruptnesses and discontinuities in the flux of personal life, but he placed them against a background of ordered and intelligible reality.

Kierkegaard, however, seems to find special worth in what is "discontinuous" and particular virtue in disorder. The net result is that his argument touches not so much our minds or our intelligently percipient emotions as our bodies, since it is aimed at our psychopathic feelings of abject creaturehood, fear, and dread. It is hardly an accident that the modern cult of "existentialism," which claims him as its forerunner, teaches an atheistic skepticism that he himself would have abhorred.

There remains a sense in which subjectivity seems particularly to be the truth for college students. The experiences of college come at a romantic time of life when feeling runs high, introspection goes deep, and a favorite ethical maxim is "To thine own self be true." The gulf between the inner life and the entire outside world is never more wide than in youth, and the impossibility of overcoming it is never more clearly seen. Many of the problems of college instruction come from our own forgetfulness as teachers of the extreme individualism of college years. The very fact that in later life the emotions make less of an uproar and that we have—alas—worked our way into a sort of stolid indifference on many issues tends to make us unaware of the tight little universes with their seething tides in which our students are confined. It is not that they are wholly unable to get out of themselves. When the right cause comes along they are quick to yield to it all that they have. But they tend to respond, I think, not so much to the reasonableness of a presented idea as to a vivid picture of misery or injustice which kindles their feelings.

The moral for our religious life is that we should respect the privacy of personal emotion and should also try to supplement it. We live in our own little worlds but fortunately not in them only. Through the rhythms of experience we move from inner to outer life, from romantic sensitivity to participation in the more obviously shared values of classical form. Strictly speaking, subjectivity is the truth only in the sense that it is the truth for the time being. We plunge into the life within but not permanently. *"Verweile doch, du bist so schön,"* cried Faust to the fleeting moment of romantic attraction. But Goethe himself, romanticist that he was, would not allow Faust to stay there. The Earth Spirit made its own broad hints to Faust that man does not live by instinct alone. And the famous cry, quoted so eagerly by the romantics, *"Grau, theurer Freund, ist alle Theorie, und grün des Lebens goldner Baum,"* is uttered by Mephistopheles, who was the devil incarnate. In the second part of the drama Faust finally falls in love with Helen. This is not just one more affair, a rebound from the attachment to Margaret. Helen, as Santayana reminds us, came originally from Sparta, the place of discipline. And Faust's love for her represents Goethe's own love for Hellas, where life was brought under the pattern of reasonable ideas. Not until he has caught the vision of beauty as abstract and enduring form is Faust ready for the constructive work of rebuilding the wasteland in which he engages before the drama ends. Only then does he perceive what the dialectic of experience means.

We do not need to stop with the incommunicable nor do we require that a miracle rescue us—this is the conclusion. The life of reason makes its own provision for excursions into the unconscious and has its own safeguards against their abuse. Interestingly enough, Kierkegaard teaches this through his personal example. By watching what he did we gain a lesson more important than the one he meant to teach. For the fact is that with all his vagaries Kierkegaard is still a great figure who throws light on the problem of the relation of reason to religion. He meant to show the failure of words and arguments where private insight is concerned. Actually he demonstrated their power to stimulate reflection and insight. He professed little interest in artistic or literary expression. But one cannot read about the romantic period in his own life without seeing how completely he depended on creative work for his mental health. So long as his tumultuous emotions were unexpressed they turned into unhealthily exaggerated enthusiasms or morbid depression. When they found outlet in literary creation they became great art and today they help a puzzled generation to understand the beauty of the religious life. Like Goethe, also, Kierkegaard found release from the urgency of romantic passion through the contemplation of classical form. We know that his favorite composer was the serene, objective Mozart.

What he really teaches, therefore, is a religion that is not the denial but the fruition of the powers of man. And he is able to teach it because he became what he tried to avoid becoming—a discerning psychologist and an artist of great skill. In spite of himself he demonstrated the faith of a man of culture, the religion of a person whose interests were broadly humane. The weight of his testimony is in favor of the belief that where sensitiveness and understanding are concerned Jesus came not to destroy but to fulfill.

If Kierkegaard, interpreted in this way, has so much to give us we should also remember that the neo-orthodox have themselves many special insights that we may not ignore. To be reasonable in religious matters is not easy, and they are right when they show that much of our so-called appeal to rationality evades the deeper and more difficult questions. They are correct in saying that our ethical choices are more complex than we often suppose. They are well grounded also when they insist that our hold on truth is often not so objective as we think and that our reason is frequently nothing but a tool for our selfishness. It is unhappily true both that our love is tainted by egoism and that its effectiveness is hampered by conditions which force it to compromise. The sad fact is that much of the time we have been fooling ourselves. As college men and women, for example, we think that we are lovers of beauty and truth, when actually we are enjoying the snobbishness of membership in an aristocratic society. We think that we are socially idealistic when as a matter of fact our mode of life exploits other men and keeps them in economic bondage. We share the terrible guilt of the war, and although we admire the courage of our pacifistic brethren we have to say that even they are caught in a competitive system where the attempt to be aloof too often brings help to the wrong side. In other words, the neo-orthodox are correct when they show that our choices are beset with ambiguities. They are less helpful, I think, when they try to point the way out. Neo-orthodoxy has undermined our confidence at a time when it needed renewal. It has exploited the tragic facts of life, a background shared by all philosophies, for special purposes of its own. It has criticized our pride but has not taught us humility. It has used argument in attacking reason. It has told us to rely on God but has cut off our access to him.

The truth is that instead of doubting reason we should learn to trust its religious efficacy. We may not give up the effort to apply it even though the results so far have been meager. We may not even relinquish faith in ourselves for, unworthy as we are, God has at present no other instruments for carrying out the particular task assigned us. What we most deeply need is insight into the supplementary roles that faith and reason play. By taking account of the natural rhythms of life we can use reason to save ourselves from helpless subjectivity and can also use faith to furnish the material on which our processes of discrimination may work. We can even prepare ourselves to face reasonably the fact of mystery and to make our experience of the unknown a source of power for greater control over the known. And in doing this we should actually be able to join hands with our neo-orthodox friends across the barriers of controversy. For the application of reason along these lines is, we would claim, in harmony with the deepest insights of the Biblical tradition.

The next lecture will turn to the Old Testament prophets for evidence.

III. A Faith That Fulfills

WE BEGAN by asking what our colleges must do to be saved. The inquiry led us to consider the differences between the faith of our fathers and that of modern times. We came to the conclusion that the changes that have occurred are the result of the new and aggressive role played by reason. A faith that is to endure must make its peace with reason and allow its tests to be applied wherever they are relevant.

At this point we turned aside to consider the claim of the neo-orthodox that the older belief in a supernatural revelation which transcends reason may be retained today practically unchanged. Kierkegaard's defense of this view interested us particularly. We found that with much of what Kierkegaard and the neo-orthodox have to say no one can disagree. They have shown conclusively how mixed are our motives and how ambiguous many of the choices life forces on us. Their emphasis on the need for action helps to drive home, also, the obvious but often forgotten truth that the right to praise and even to hold ideals must be earned in the sphere of deeds.

Yet ultimately their theology fails to help modern man at the crucial point. He is puzzled because he does not know just where faith comes in or how it should be related to the rest of his mental life. The neo-orthodox say that it comes abruptly, bringing discontinuity, and they seem to revel in the rift it creates. Opposed to this is our view that faith and reason enter into a partnership that is harmonious since faith is active commitment to the Rational Good. To show that this view of religion can find Biblical support let us now turn to the Old Testament prophets and in particular to Micah's famous statement of what religious loyalty means. It is especially relevant because upon analysis it reveals its own illustrations of the rhythm of the religious life referred to earlier and shows some of the forms it assumes as spiritual insight develops. "He hath showed thee, O man, what is good," you will recall that Micah cried; "and what doth the Lord require of thee, but to do justly, and to love mercy, and to walk humbly with thy God?"

Recently one of my friends remarked in conversation: "If the churches have no more to offer than these words of Micah they will do well to close their doors entirely." His meaning was that this is not religion but morality. At about the time of this conversation I read a review of a recent book on the Old Testament prophets. "The writer states their process of reasoning," said the reviewer, "but the powerful act of God is not brought home to the reader." The review went on to say that the book failed to show that it was the experience in which they were "taken hold of by God himself in a forceful way" that made the prophets important. The comment set me to wondering. "How can God take hold of us in a forceful way," I asked myself, "if not through reasonable ideas reinforced by the feelings that our human relationships have shown to be good? That God is not the same as human beings is clear. But can reason and love be essentially different for Him from what they are for us? Does not the real religious insight of the prophets come from their awareness of the deeper ranges of authority that these qualities themselves can be shown to have?"

With this question in mind let us look at Micah's idea of religion. First of all we notice that he offers some general rules—do justly, he says, love mercy—and this gives us pause, for generalities are out of favor in our present climate of opinion. Not only the neo-orthodox, but a host of critics with long and forbidding names—we call them semanticists, positivists, pragmatists, and operationalists—press upon us the advantages of the specific and concrete. Of what use, they ask, is it for Micah to say let justice be done, when the real question is: What particular acts does justice require? How, for example, does one deal justly with the demands of an enemy in a war—cold or hot? And what does it mean to love mercy when hostilities are at an advanced stage? Again, can we be asked both to do justly and to love mercy when everybody knows that often one cancels out the other? As for "walking humbly with God"—the phrase is preposterously vague until we know more about what God himself is like.

Obviously the criticism has some merit. We face many situations where the real difficulty is to know not what new principle to adopt but how to use the principles already in hand. And in a scientific age an abstract idea like justice has trouble in establishing its own status. It is not an empirical datum. We cannot see, touch, or feel it. We are unable to take it into the laboratory or to assign it a place in our knowledge of the physical world. Yet there are certain things it does accomplish for us. It serves as a reminder of a type of action that we have reflectively chosen as good. It stands for a quality that fits reasonably into place with other considered standards of conduct. And although in a given situation it may not itself present new facts, it does point to the place where such facts will be found. It will not always tell us exactly what to do but it will tell us where to go to find out what to do. In this sense it has authority for us.

Micah's appeal to justice, then, was to an idea which, though it may have no power in itself, must be invoked, along with specific knowledge, if certain issues are to be settled rightly. His appeal to so abstract a conception in the name of God was, further, to suggest that God's authority is of the kind that the rational mind recognizes. For we should notice that it is characteristic of rationality to respond to general rules as such. We see this most easily when we contrast human with subhuman experience. To an animal, for example, an object is something to be seized or avoided, an immediate stimulus to appetite or to fear. Like an animal, primitive man appears also to live much of the time in the world of the here and now. If we read the record rightly he finds his first glimmerings of another world in his experience of the taboo, which tells him that something must *never* be done and that a certain type of act is *always* wrong. The taboo is often criticized by modern scholars because it is so very general and so free from specific distinctions. It applies to all kinds of acts and objects, good and bad alike, and seems often to be lost in a haze of nonmoral obscurity. Yet although it is true that the practical and moral effect of some taboos is bad, it remains a fact that the generality inherent in the idea of the unbreakable rule played its part in the developing role of mind. To be aware of the universal is to take a step forward into the distinctive world of reason. Only the rational mind can free itself from enslavement to the immediate. It alone is able to recognize the binding force of that which is everywhere and always true. Micah's appeal to general truths in the name of God shows his insight into the fact that the authority of reason and that of religion coalesce at least in one area. To say that God requires men to observe the law of justice is to say that God's commands use the form that only a rational mind can understand.

The first point to notice, then, is that Micah's use of general ideas is not necessarily a way of evading decisions but is evidence of his belief that, whatever else God may be, he is Lord of the realm of mind. Let us note, secondly, that in his stress on justice Micah chooses a particularly apt illustration, for of all values justice most closely resembles reason in the type of authority to which it appeals. To see why this is so let us turn to the prophet by whose views of justice Micah was undoubtedly influenced. Shortly before Micah, the prophet Amos came from the wilderness of Tekoa to tell the priests at Bethel how far they had strayed from the path to God. Amos was a man of passion but he was no fanatic. It is true that he described his call to be a prophet as a sudden overpowering feeling. "The lion hath roared," he said, to illustrate the irresistible quality of God's message, "who [then] will not fear? The Lord God hath spoken, who can but prophesy?" At first this sounds like the emotional assurance of dogmatism. But as we examine Amos's teaching we see that what lay back of these words was a conviction of the demonstrable rightness of the religious view. The prophet was indeed "taken hold of by God in a forceful way," to use our reviewer's words, but the ultimate source of God's power, as Amos saw it, was not arbitrary.

Consider the musical form his words take: "Shall horses run upon the rock? will one plow there with oxen? for ye have turned judgment into gall, and the fruit of righteousness into hemlock." "Hear this, O ye that swallow up the needy, even to make the poor of the land to fail, saying, When will the new moon be gone, that we may sell corn? and the sabbath, that we may set forth wheat, making the ephah small, and the shekel great, and falsifying the balances by deceit? that we may buy the poor for silver, and the needy for a pair of shoes; yea, and sell the refuse of the wheat?" This, I submit, is the utterance of a musician. For an unlettered herdsman whom God called as he followed the flock, the continuous flow of the patterned and harmonious cadences is remarkable. Amos was primarily a poet, with a poet's sense for balanced form. He could not have prophesied as he did if he had not had an artist's feeling for the demands of rhythm and proportion.

Now let us press the point a step further. Was it not this same feeling for balance in the arrangement of the parts of the social organism that influenced his sensitiveness to the demand of God for justice? He inveighed against ritual, but it was not ritual as such that bothered him. What was wrong was the use of ritual to enhance the power of the few at the expense of the many and so to throw the social scales out of line. "I hate, I despise your feast days," said God as Amos heard him. The reason was not that feasts or Sabbaths or new moons were bad in themselves but that some people had used them to curry special favor with the divine. In Amos's time the sacred had come to be identified with that which was out of the ordinary. It was the unusual day such as the Sabbath, the man with unusual work such as the priest, the unusual experience such as the prophetic seizure, the unusual and untestable vision of the irrational dogmatist which proclaimed the presence of God. In Elijah's age this emphasis on the unusual went so far that on occasions religion was completely divorced from reasonable ethics and God was even supposed to have sent to Ahab's court a lying prophet whose sacredness consisted merely in his insane frenzy.

Amos saw that this attitude was wrong not only because it undermined men's ideas of integrity but because it identified God's ways with the life of the favored few. Opposing this identification he proclaimed justice because it stood for a universal human value where all men shared alike. Justice for him, as for Plato, meant the health of the social organism, the perfect balance of its parts won through the harmonious and co-operative activity of all groups. Indeed, Amos's passion for the universal drove him to what for his contemporaries must have been a desperately radical conclusion. "Are ye not as the children of the Ethiopians unto me?" he heard God say. "Have not I brought up Israel out of the land of Egypt? *and* the Philistines from Caphtor, *and* the Syrians from Kir?" Don't trade any more on your special relations with God, said Amos in effect, for other nations have been chosen as well as you. God's will works without favoritism and in accordance with a consistent formal pattern that is as wide as the universe itself.

Of course for Amos God was much more than an ideal form revealing himself in the patterns of beauty, justice, and reason; he was also an active force in nature and history. The rhythms of nature Amos found tremendously impressive. "Seek him that maketh the seven stars and Orion, and turneth the shadow of death into the morning, and maketh the day dark with night; that calleth for the waters of the sea, and poureth them out upon the face of the earth." The same force was at work as inexorably in the affairs of men. "Let judgment roll down as waters, and righteousness as a mighty stream."

At this point questions arise. Amos's figure was somewhat inexact, was it not? Does justice roll down as waters? It can hardly have the effect of a force like gravitation, for if it is inevitable it cannot be justice. The difference is that between a mechanical and a reasonable sequence. The planets move automatically by gravitational pull. This means that they cannot make mistakes. Wherever they are it is "right" that they should be there in the only sense in which right can be applied to them. But with rational beings the case is different.

They can make mistakes and they can go to places where it is not right for them to be. Yet the fact that they can wander makes their achievement when they do go straight of incomparably greater significance.

What, then, is the law of justice? The problem how a reasonable creative will could be expected to work either in nature or in and through the freedom of human personal life is not an easy one to solve from any point of view. But Amos shows that at least for human minds the reasonable ideal has its own type of compulsion. The rational will is free but its decisions are not arbitrary. It is not free to flout the authority of reason. It is not free even to question reason for in the very act of questioning it presupposes that which it would deny. In this sense reason's authority is absolute. Is not the same true of justice? Amos, for his part, was sure that it was effectively at work in history to destroy the erring nation. We find it hard to share his confidence as we see the wicked prosper and the righteous suffer. But actually the influence of justice does not rest on its ability to keep men from being unjust any more than that of reason comes from its power to prevent the irrational. Justice is a standard for action. It has no mechanical attraction, but it sets forth a claim that the reasonable mind cannot deny. The demand for equality among persons is basically the same as the demand of the principle of coherence for equality among facts.

God works on man through the lure of reason and justice. His authority is inevitable though his purposes are often thwarted. But how does he work on physical nature? Does it also respond to the lure of the ideal? Here we face one of those philosophical discussions that appear to have no end. I think it can at least be said, however, that if the believer in the divine reason has trouble explaining how it can work both in nature and in history, his opponent is no better off. No theologian, whatever his shade of opinion, finds it easy to show just why God does what he does. Certainly Kierkegaard is not helpful when he argues, as he seems to, that God's will works unreasonably. And there are signs' that something like reason is effectively at work in the whole evolutionary process. As we study it we see many evidences of the influence of a form-bringing tendency. From the gravitational and electromagnetic fields at the physical level, on through the periodicity of the elements in chemistry and the remarkable properties won by the biological organism through its advanced sensitiveness to pattern, this trend has brought about the marvelous flexibility of the human nervous system and brain. The next step, difficult in practice but clearly required by the logic of the developing process, is toward an international organization. Throughout organic evolution what we see is an influence, similar, at least, to ideas, which takes us in the direction of patterns that in their increasing complexity make progressively implausible any theory that omits the factor of mind.

Of course it has often been said that even on the plane of human affairs reason is not the lure of the ideal, as we have pictured it, but simply a very practical device worked out by men on this planet to help them get the food, shelter, and weapons they wanted. Instead of standing for the harmonious and the co-operative it represents a tool developed in the stress of competition as a means of insuring survival. But opposed to this view is what seems to me the profounder attitude which holds that reason and justice should be obeyed not because they are useful but because as reason and justice they have distinctive claims of their own. Reason does help us to get our own way, but this is not its real significance. Essentially it provides us with abstract ideas which, as we saw earlier, relieve us from the thralldom of the here and now. It gives us the universality and necessity of logic with its rules that everywhere and in all circumstances are valid. It introduces us to the irresistible demand of the network of relations we call coherent. In this way it opens our eyes to the presence of an intrinsic value, an end in itself whose worth we are unable to deny or even to question, and whose claim we recognize even when we think we flout it. Because it confronts us with this final authority we can only believe that it brings us into the presence of God.

To say this is, however, to show the need of saying more. Human experience is obviously much more than the collecting of facts and the careful analyzing of their formal relations. Just as obviously God is more than God of the intellect. Reason's forms are abstract. They reach out for the warm rich content of human feeling. As if the muse of history sensed this need and wished to clothe with living flesh the bare bones of Amos's thought, there appeared in his own century his remarkable younger contemporary Hosea. "What doth the Lord require of thee," you will recall that Micah asked, "but to do justly and love mercy?" As unforgettable as Amos's description of justice is Hosea's account of what mercy means.

To read Hosea is to realize that his revolt against the view of religion as the property of a special group is as marked as in the case of Amos, although his approach is totally different. Amos dealt with abstract form; Hosea examines palpitating feeling in all its agony. Where Amos's imagination roamed over the wide sweep of nature and history, Hosea probes the depths of the individual human heart. Amos's vision is broader, but the insight of Hosea goes deeper. Amos is like the scientist who draws general conclusions from watching particular events in nature; Hosea is like the artist in being able to take the single instance as characteristic of the universal. Amos appeals to the rule of reason, Hosea to the most intimate of emotional experiences, where reason is completely at a discount, namely, infidelity in marriage. Hosea found that his wife was unfaithful, yet to his amazement he loved her still and with God's blessing took her back. As he touched bedrock in his own feelings he discovered not what was peculiar to himself but what was basic for all human life.

Notice his means of approach to his people. I speak to you, he said in effect, not from a special office, not as prophet or priest or prince—though he might have claimed to be all three—not even as Jew, on the basis of our favored experience as a nation, but rather as husband and father and therefore as man to man. I am talking, he continued to say in effect, out of the background of the family relation into which all men are born. I say to you that just as surely as men love they must suffer but that this need not lead to private grief or the exclusiveness of despair. Accepted in the right spirit it brings insight into the qualities that bind men to each other and to their God. Suffering must characterize the experience of God himself if he is a God of love. It is in suffering that we enter most intimately into our neighbor's mind and also see most clearly the nature of him whom we serve. As the Spanish philosopher Unamuno said, many centuries later, "Suffering is that which unites all living beings together; it is the universal or divine blood that flows through us all."

If you have read *The Green Pastures* you may recall the place where the Lord comes down from heaven to watch the siege of Jerusalem and to talk with the defenders of the city. On one of the fortifications he finds a non-Biblical and nonhistorical but very real character named Hezdrel and asks for whom he is fighting. Hezdrel replies that he and the others are fighting for Hosea's deity, the God of love who suffers with his people, and that he has little interest in the older God of wrath. I think the author is right in emphasizing that this is a new God. The God of Abraham, invoked by Kierkegaard, was not strictly a God of love, nor was He a God who suffered, and He was certainly a God of one particular tribe. As the Hebrew genius explored the possibilities of this problem it developed ideas which must have seemed revolutionary but which have stood up under the test of time. Amos was only one of several who were groping for the idea of a universal God. He reached it through his passion for justice. Hosea represents a different group, but its influence was to be as lasting.

Notice if you will that Amos and Hosea together exemplify not only the appeal to the universal as the true basis for religion but also the polarity of life as it takes account now of one goal, now of another that supplements it. In actual experience do we not appeal to both prophets, contradictory though they may at first seem to be? Justice and mercy appear to set up differing standards, yet in the rhythm of life what we do is to determine what is theoretically just and then, as we treat the particular case, try to view with sympathy its special circumstances. The alternation is similar to what takes place in the process of knowing. As the rationalists have shown, we must seek on the one hand the clear outlines of logical analysis. But in doing so we leave the flux of empirical phenomena behind. To this we must return if experience is not to be barren. We cannot remain with the rational pattern of Descartes, for this would mean dalliance in the realm of the abstractly formal. No more can we spend all our time with Bergson's passing show, for while concepts without percepts are empty, percepts without concepts are blind. I am inclined to think that especially at a time of widespread suffering like the present we need to take account of still another type of rhythm, to which Hosea's teaching points. It has to do with our relation to the fact of pain in the world at large. We seek peace of mind for ourselves yet we cannot win it except by leaving the thought of suffering behind. A kind of forgetfulness of the world's agony is needed, it would seem, if we would keep our sanity. The forgetfulness, however, may not be permanent. To suffering we must return, not only as an experience to undergo but as a datum for reflection and a theme to ponder.

This brings us to the third phrase in Micah's definition and a further use of the principle of alternation. What doth the Lord require of us but to do justly with Amos, to love mercy with Hosea, and to walk humbly in the spirit of the great prophet who was Micah's older contemporary, namely, Isaiah? Isaiah knew better than most people the meaning of humility before God because his own ideas of it went through such a radical change. As the prophet who agonized over the fact of mystery he faces us with the question whether, like suffering, mystery may not be a recurrent datum in experience, to which we continually return but with which we cannot rest.

You will recall that in the sixth chapter of the book bearing his name he tells us that he saw the Lord high and lifted up, surrounded by seraphim who cried "Holy, Holy, Holy." As he gazed, the posts of the door moved and the house was filled with smoke. To our minds seraphs and cherubs are pleasant little cupids or angels. We must remember, however, that for a Jew of the eighth century B.C. they were monstrous creatures in every sense of the word. They were both huge and abnormal, with human heads, animal bodies, and menacing wings. The word "holy," further, meant not righteous and good, as it does to us, but apart, mysterious, and terrifying. What the seraphs really cried was "taboo." Isaiah's response was that of primitive man who feels that he has looked upon the terrible sacred object and therefore must die.

"Woe is me," he cried, "for I am undone; because I am a man of unclean lips and I dwell in the midst of a people of unclean lips." His meaning was that he had not gone through the proper ritual to stand in the presence of the literally awful religious object. God was the mysterious "Wholly Other" whose authority was based on fear. Then comes a change almost startling in its completeness. It took hundreds of years for the minds of his countrymen to absorb it but Isaiah talks as though it happened to him in the twinkling of an eye. He says that a seraph touched his lips with a live coal from the altar. Immediately he saw that this was a God he could understand and could serve with love. When, therefore, God said: "Whom shall I send and who will go for us?" his response was that of a loyal follower and *believer*: "Here am I, send me."

At this point, it seems to me, we watch one of the greatest transitions in intellectual and religious history. It has happened more than once in the life of a nation. In happens constantly in the experience of the man of faith. The mysterious and uncharted areas of experience, to use Gilbert Murray's phrase, surround us on every side. Toward them we must take some attitude. As Professor Murray says, we reach out to them using our most sensitive feelers and tentacles. We turn to ritual because it brings a feeling of the sublime, we design our churches to suggest the mysterious unknown, we gaze at the starry heavens to recover our feelings for infinity.

But the important point to notice is that we do not stay with the mystery. Like Isaiah we find that the call of the unknown is ultimately the call of fear. God as the object of our reasonable loyalty must have more to say to us than this. So we begin to realize, as did Isaiah, that God's difference from man, basically, is not the difference of the unknown from the known but of the moral ideal in its purity from man's feeble efforts to attain it. The difference can never be overcome, but within limits it can progressively be made less if man will exert himself morally. We return to the mystery both because it is infallibly there and also because it exerts its own peculiar lure and stimulus. But we continually make the discovery that neither the other-than-man nor the greater-than-man-in-power is the rightful object of our worship. Sheer power means sheer physical strength or sheer force such as that of gravitational pull. In itself it has no moral quality. But because in worship the sense for power leads on beyond itself to the sense for spiritual power, and the feeling for what is other than man blends into the feeling for what is greater than man's present moral achievement, the experience becomes religiously satisfactory. The most impressive polarity in worship is that of mystery and value. But value must have the last word for it is value alone that is rationally significant. God is greater than we but the greatness is of a sort we know and respect and find good. His difference is not in kind or such as to put him and our whole relation to him completely beyond our comprehension. If God is the rational and ethical ideal we can, however imperfectly, make his will our own, and can co-operate, however unworthily, in the effort to carry out his purpose. In this sense we can walk humbly with our God.

It seems to me, therefore, that Micah's combination of Amos's passion for justice, Hosea's love of mercy, and Isaiah's sensitiveness to humility gives us a definition of religion that satisfies the profound demands of feeling without violating the exacting claims of logical consistency. It shows us in the first place that the appeal to abstract ideas need not be as vain as is sometimes supposed. Often we hear it said that Sanskrit as a language of independent clauses connected by *ands* is significant of Hindu indifference to history. Hindu myths unfold in recurrent cycles or in dreams of the god Brahman where all ideas have the same status, there are no subordinate clauses, and development or progress in time has no meaning. In the same way it is remarked of the

Hebrew mind and language that they are geared to the unfolding of a historical purpose in time. Superficially this definition of Micah's may seem to belong to the Sanskrit rather than the Hebrew world.

But even our brief analysis is sufficient to show that Micah's insights are no timeless essences unrelated to the stream of human events. They were forged in the fires of struggle. They represent the crystallization of feelings that have faced up to the ultimate crises of life and death. General in form, they yet are directly relevant to the particular facts of daily living. And when placed in their historical setting they illustrate vividly the restless rhythmic character of the human quest for religious insight. For whether the pendulum swings between mercy and justice or between mystery and value it is clear that the private resources of feeling and the more open and public methods of reason must supplement each other when the goal of our strivings is God.

Too often man thinks of himself as standing alone in a world that is either indifferent to his values or actually irrational and as placed in a universe where anything resembling a divine event toward which the whole creation moves is desperately hard to discover. Yet he cannot doubt that within his own mind there is a desire for order. Nor can he doubt that in addition to its wayward impulses his own heart reveals the more constructive purposes of love. And as he studies the conditions in which his purposes thrive he becomes aware of an insistent demand laid on him that he can in no wise escape or deny. It does not come merely from himself for it imposes a reasonable will of its own. Standing over against his desires and prescribing the course his purposes should follow is a network of relations which the most sensitive members of the race have taken as evidence of the presence of justice, mercy, and humility as norms for right living. To know this gives modern man a conviction of the bond that unites him with kindred spirits in his own and other lands, in his own age and in ages that have passed. And the fact that some of these can speak across the centuries, bearing their own testimony to the reality of the unseen source of these standards strengthens his assurance that he and humanity are not alone.

IV. The Ministry of Pain

To THE troubling conclusion that the more we learn about nature and man the less we know about God the modern mind has come. Yet to reach such a conclusion is to find it contradictory. If there is a God all our knowledge must in some sense come from him. And to know the truth about our world and ourselves should mean knowing the truth about God. The only way to doubt this would be to say with Kierkegaard that God is separated from us by some chasm that needs a supernatural bridge. We saw, however, that to make such an appeal to the "supernatural" is to raise problems rather than to solve them because the term itself is so hard to understand. The one intelligible attempt to give it significance is that made by the philosophical idealists who sometimes use the word to designate that which is above nature, as reason is. In such a context, however, it becomes merely a synonym for "rational."

Turning away from the supernatural we went accordingly to some of the more familiar figures in the prophetic tradition of the Old Testament. As we looked at them we discovered that their flaming religious insights and their active passion for social reform expressed the fulfillment of reason in their experience rather than its denial. These prophets did things that appeared miraculous and they probably believed in miracles themselves. But as we studied them we saw that the law they really appealed to was that of reason and that their magnificent effectiveness came from the harmonious relationship their sensitive hearts were able to establish with their orderly minds. Even where they confronted the unknown they were able to make their experience of it contribute to rationally purposeful action. Their power seems to have come at least in part from their mastery of the natural rhythms of reason and faith and their ability to give each type of experience its due. When it was time to feel deeply they surrendered to the promptings of the heart, and when analysis and criticism were called for they were used without compromise. Each phase of life enriched the other.

We have said that the prophets felt deeply. One of the most frequent criticisms directed at a faith which attempts to be rational is that it lacks the warmth of the deeper emotions. Our present discussion and the one following will attempt to meet this criticism by exploring two areas of feeling on which a rational faith may draw for content. Few experiences, if any, go deeper than our awareness of pain and few if any are more ecstatic than our awareness of beauty. Let us take these two types of experience, then, as examples of feeling that is powerful without being irrational. And as we study them let us remember that to attempt to be reasonable in our thought about God does not mean to be free from emotional stress. On the contrary, we cannot think about him adequately unless our feelings are profoundly stirred.

In this lecture we shall turn to that bitterest of all human problems for our feeling and most difficult for our thought— the question of the meaning of pain and its relation to our ideas about God. For the older generation as for the modern neo-orthodox the problem of pain is inseparably associated with that of sin. The first question we face, then, is whether we need this association. It seems at times as though neo-orthodox writers were trying to bring the idea of sin back into prominence as a means of appealing to our feelings. But are there not other ideas that will do the job better? No one will deny that man is sinful in the sense that he is lazy, ignorant, full of lust and greed, and that this is at the root of all our difficulties. But do we need this emphasis on Sin with a capital S? Are there not better ways of cultivating the humble and contrite heart?

We should notice in the first place that the word "sin" is what the grammarians would call a hortatory term and is used to arouse emotion rather than to communicate ideas. At a certain stage in his religious experience the suppliant is bound to exclaim, "Father, I have sinned against heaven and in thy sight." He does this, however, not to convey information to God or to anyone else. The cry is that of a man standing afar off who will not lift up so much as his eyes unto heaven but who, smiting his breast and peering into the dark recesses of his inner life, says: "God be merciful to me." It is an utterance straight from the heart, addressed to the heart of God, and as such is private, personal, and not intended as a shared or communicated experience in the usual meaning of those words.

The point becomes more clear when we see the resistance the term "sin" offers to its use in any universal sense. We may say of our neighbor that he has faults or shortcomings or that he makes mistakes, and the remark, although impolite, may be relevant, significant, and true. But to say of him that he sins is something else. "Sin" is an emotionally charged term which we use of others at our peril and at the peril of failing to clarify our own meanings. Furthermore, there are certain great individuals whom you and I have in mind who are so free from the taint of the usual human egoism and selfishness that for us to call them sinful would be outrageous. At the very thought of such a thing our feelings rise in revolt. Obviously we are dealing here with a term that refuses to fit our usual categories of communicable discourse and takes its place apart as a word to conjure with, perhaps, but not to convey an intelligible meaning.

In the second place, we should see that the modern writer does not really have the same feeling for sin as did his forebears. Try as he will, the modern thinker simply cannot escape the fact that along with all who live in the contemporary world he is tarred with the liberal brush. We have seen before that he does not take the Bible as a completely authoritarian document. Actually he selects from it those parts he believes can be justified as true—a procedure his theological predecessors never could have understood. They were born into an authoritarian tradition and had no doubts about the ineradicable nature of sin. They were brought up in surroundings where such a feeling was taken for granted, and whatever misgivings they had about it were not of an intellectual sort. If I am not much mistaken the sense of sin of the moderns is far more sophisticated. It has become a theme for the esoteric poet with his following of baffled but believing readers or the disillusioned theologian who in his revolt against liberalism has reached into the past to find props for his creed. Thus there is an element of artificiality and make-believe in the way it is used. The present sense of sin is one we argue ourselves into instead of accepting naturally, inevitably, and on the basis of an unquestioned authority.

In the third place, the modern treatment of sin is made ambiguous by the change in our notion of God's justice and judgment. Neo-orthodox writers talk about the judgment of history as an expression of God's will. What do they really mean? Is it actually their belief that God visits the sins of the fathers on the children unto the third and fourth generation? Even in the time of Jeremiah and Ezekiel men knew better.

That children suffer for the sins of fathers is tragically true. That this is the will of God and expresses his purpose is impossible to believe if God wills either justice or love. Our fathers feared a day of wrath when their sins would be uncovered. We are told to look for a day of judgment when the nations will be called to account. Can anyone claim that the two are morally similar? To punish civilization as a whole is not to mete out justice to the individual. By any intelligible standard of justice the "punishment" suffered by millions of individuals in this or any other war was preposterously out of line with any sins they had committed. Nor is the matter made easier by the appeal to "God's justice" rather than ours. Once again we face the fact that the word "sin" applies to the individual in his Maker's presence and nowhere else.

In the fourth place, one has only to observe the terrible effects on persons of nervous instability when too much is made of "sin," and the ease with which the word is associated with morbid introspection to see that we have here a conception of dubious religious value. Says a prominent psychologist: Children brought up to believe they are sinful come to "despise, distrust, and even hate themselves." There must be better and truer ways, one feels, of stimulating the will and sensitizing the feelings than by resorting to this device with all the problems it brings in its train. The fact is that an emphasis on sin plunges us once again into the subjectivity of Kierkegaard and does so just at the time in history when as individuals and as a society we need to be freed from excessive preoccupation with ourselves and given goals to work for that are both good and within our grasp. The motives of those who stress this point are of course easy to understand. They want, as they say, to make our theological point of view more inclusive and profound. We can agree with them that the horrors of recent years have literally shocked us not only out of all complacency but out of the confidence our technical advances had created. It is true that we need a theology that will minister to the bitterness of our disillusionment. But this return to Calvinism and renewal of a Calvinistic emphasis on sin will not give it to us. It fails to offer the kind of depth we need and it affords us no help in facing the future. With its insistence that something is *ineradicably* and *unchangeably* wrong it takes away such confidence as we have left. And its appeal to supernatural grace revealed exclusively in one historical tradition raises two obstacles. First, it brings up all the old questions as to what supernaturalism really means. Second, it puts the emphasis on the idea of a chosen people and an unshared revelation at just the time in history when the conception of a God of our common life is beginning to emerge from the divisions of sectarian provincialism. As a topic for introspection, then, sin fails to stimulate the energies of the heart while as a theological doctrine it is unable to answer the inquiries of the mind. Surely our religious thought can do better as it reaches out for suggestions in this our hour of need.

Perhaps the answer will be found in a new treatment of the age-old experience of pain. If we go at it in the right way can we not find in it new constructive possibilities for our thought? The suffering of human beings is a grievous fact. Understandably we shrink from it and put it out of our minds just as we try to keep from thinking about hospital and cemetery. We must agree that it has its own dangerous leanings toward morbid sentimentality and psychopathic dread. Yet, personal and introspective as are the emotions it arouses, can they not be made into a bridge that will take us out of our own subjectivity into a larger and more humane point of view? The experience of pain reaches far enough into the innermost depths to satisfy even Kierkegaard. But instead of calling up all the problems of an authoritarian theology it seems to reveal the larger perspectives and to disclose the conditions against which as a background all human life is carried on. We have seen how Hosea used it to make clear the bond that unites all men at the deeper levels of existence. The fact is that the problems of suffering rise from the profounder levels of the collective experience of the race and have never presented themselves with a greater urgency than in the day in which we live.

Sin, then, is an experience that drives the individual in upon his own privacy. Suffering, on the other hand, is universally shared. All men suffer, some of them most of the time. It is of course claimed that all men also sin, but for the reasons noted this is not so unambiguously clear. The same people whom it is so hard to call sinful obviously suffer; indeed, often they suffer most of all. The fact is that suffering has an inclusiveness that appals us when we stop to reflect on it.

In the next place, the idea of sin is treated in detail by only one of the great historical religions, whereas the idea of suffering is central in several. Of course one may be right and the others wrong. But our growing awareness of the amount of insight that is embodied in other traditions than our own leads us to wonder whether the larger agreement may not mean the deeper wisdom. Of the relation between sin and suffering in Christianity itself Charles Péguy has written:

> The Son has taken upon himself all the sins of the world
> And the mother all the grief.

Does this comment not carry a suggestion that grief is the all-enfolding emotion? Is not the suffering of the mother the more inclusive? The mother's experience includes the pain both of birth and of death. There is a sense in which suffering seems to span the complete arc of life and to overreach even the experience of redemption of sin. This all-encompassing quality, symbolized in the eternally sorrowing feminine, helps us to understand the adoration not only of the Virgin Mary but of the Great Mother in Asia Minor or the compassionate Kuan Yin in China. The spectacle of suffering, either human or divine, draws us together. We are united by the sorrowing experience of the great soul wherever we find it—witness the effect on us, who do not believe him to be a god, of the sensitive Gautama under the bo tree in India, or the semireligious cult in our own country of Lincoln, who suffered so visibly under the tragedies of slavery and war. Sin raises dogmatic questions and stimulates controversy. Suffering, whether our own or that of another, breaks down the barriers of caste and creed.

In the third place, not only is suffering as an experience universal but as a problem it raises issues for the reflective mind that suggest the need for concerted action. It is the great unresolved dilemma of this and of all times and as such it is a constant stimulus, both practical and theoretical, to efforts which society as a whole must make. It is harder to account for suffering than for sin. Since human beings have the desires they do, it is not difficult to see why selfishness should be so prevalent. And although moral evil is the blacker of the two, theologians seem to have found it easy to fit it into a scheme of thought where the divine will prevails. But about the idea of suffering and its place in the larger picture there is an ever present mystery. Even the religious solution of belief in a future life where the pain of this world is made good evades the challenge. The neo-orthodox seem not to have realized this. They call on God to rescue us from the human predicament and talk about redemption on another level as if they did not see its impossibility. For how can immortality itself give a final answer? Even for it the circle remains uncompleted and the discord unresolved. In this world no restoration to freedom can really make up for the horrors of the concentration camp. No victory in war can undo the destruction war causes. Yet this kind of atonement is what we too often look for in another life, and we should see that in the nature of the case the hope is not justified. No amount of heavenly bliss can balance the account of the soldier whose death deprives him of his normal heritage and expectation as a man, nor can even heavenly love undo all the results or purify all the sordidness of earthly cruelty.

In fact, it often seems as though suffering which makes religion necessary also made it impossible. Suffering drives us to faith yet seems to keep us from accepting it, for we wonder why a good God should not shudder at the results of his own creation. The religious man is in a quandary since the same sensitiveness that sharpens his sense for values makes him also alert to disvalues. The same experiences of discrimination which prompt him to love the world for its beauty make him hate it for its ugliness. As a possibility or a general idea suffering, like evil, appears to be a necessary condition of the good life. A world without it, we say, would be morally neutral and therefore not to be desired. But what of the actual agony of the child in the presence of the screaming bomb? It is at least a question whether a world with such real events is good at all and this makes us ask whether a world with such possibilities can be good. Suffering is a problem not because it denies us what we actually and sometimes cheaply or selfishly want but because it cuts across our critically judged wants and blocks the reasonable good. Jacob Riis used to maintain that anyone who could really comprehend the misery of the slums would never smile again. Is this to argue that some kinds of understanding are themselves bad? Dostoevski puts the problem in this way:

Listen! [he makes Ivan say, in *The Brothers Karamazov*] If all must suffer to pay for the eternal harmony what have children to do with it, tell me, please? . . . I understand solidarity among men. I understand solidarity in retribution, too; but there can be no such solidarity with children. And if it is really true that they must share responsibility for all their fathers' crimes, such a truth is not of this world and is beyond my comprehension. . . . If the sufferings of children go to swell the sum of sufferings which was necessary to pay for truth, then I protest that the truth was not worth such a price. . . . And so I hasten to give back my entrance ticket, and if I am an honest man I am bound to give it back as soon as possible. And that I am doing. It's not God that I don't accept, Alyosha, only I most respectfully return him the ticket.

Does this mean that in the end suffering isolates the despairing individual from his fellows and his God? We must not evade the fact that it can and does. Suffering not only poses an insoluble problem; as an experience it sometimes dehumanizes and brutalizes. It can easily become pathological. It can oppose seemingly insuperable obstacles to the light of reason. It can quench the last glimmerings of religious hope. Jeremiah's cry: "Wilt thou be altogether as a liar unto me?" or even Amphitryon's: "Thou art a stupid god, or not an honest one" must have been wrung from the lips of many a skeptic and must have crossed the mind of many an agonized believer. Yet it is still true that this is not the characteristic human attitude. Suffering also becomes a bond. It can provide a basis for common action. We do not know why the conditions of existence should be such that men suffer as they do. We do know that the question itself loses some of its bitter insistence when theological thought gives way to practical deed, and speculation over the nature of the world yields to concern for the plight of one's neighbor. Some suffering can be transmuted through love. This is the single answer that has been found in the course of the universal search and it is one on which those who have a right to speak are in agreement.

Says Edgar in *King Lear*:

> But then the mind much sufferance doth o'erskip
> When grief hath mates and bearing fellowship.

Katherine Mansfield goes a step further. "I do not want to die," she writes in her *Journal*, "without leaving a record of my belief that suffering can be overcome. . . . Do not resist. Take it. . . . Be overwhelmed. Accept it fully. Make it *part of life*. Everything that we really accept undergoes a change. So suffering must become love. This is the mystery. This is what I must do. I must pass from personal love to greater love." In his book *The Tragic Sense of Life* Unamuno writes: "Men love one another with a spiritual love only when they have suffered the same sorrow together." Says Edwin McNeill Poteat in *Over the Sea, the Sky*:[1]

> He cannot heal who has not suffered much,
> For only Sorrow, Sorrow understands.
> They will not come for healing at our touch
> Who have not seen the scars upon our hands.

And in his inimitable way William James commented on his own grief to a friend: "It brings one closer to all mankind—this world-old experience."

It seems to me that we have not sufficiently exploited this capacity of suffering to bind us together and have not used it as we might in constructing our own religious philosophy. How, for example, can we more effectively resist a materialistic hedonism in our own minds or the minds of our students than by showing its failure to measure up to the demands that the widespread experience of suffering makes on us? And if on the practical side we are troubled by our tendency to hide in cloistered halls, whether these be on an actual physical campus or within the ivy-clad walls of our minds, how can

[1] Copyright, 1945, by Harper & Brothers and reprinted by permission.

we better drive home the urgency of moral decision than by fixing our attention on the sheer tragedy inherent in daily life?

It is clear that our young people are as ready today as ever to respond to the appeal of the sufferer and to take up arms against injustice. Indeed, the present generation of youth is probably more aware than are we of the actual extent of suffering and of its implications for our thought. A Colby student who had been a flyer in the war wrote recently in our college newspaper: "We have been part of a gigantic concerted social action and it has taught us cooperation. We have seen our buddy and our enemy die, and we have become compassionate. We have mingled with the people of Stuttgart and Manila, Norwich and Aomori, and we have at least a basis for toleration. Probably most of all we have been awakened to the problems that beset the world and we are eager to know how they can be solved."

Had he lived eighty years ago at Colby this boy could hardly have failed to join those whose records we read in an earlier lecture, and his words are an interesting hint as to what they might say to us today. Like them he has an acute sense of responsibility and a deep religious concern. But it is suffering that moves him rather than sin, and I think one can sense a difference in the result in his own mind. Am I not right in affirming that he looks outward rather than within and is caught by the claim of the common experience as much as by the introspective feeling? Both generations of students, new and old alike, are exercised over the plight of the people of Aomori and Manila. The difference, of emphasis rather than essential quality, is that the modern boy sees the problem as economic and sociological as well as religious and is calling for "gigantic concerted social action." He realizes the common human character of the problem, and one cannot read his words without feeling that in effect he is appealing to the God of our common life. Testimony like this helps to remind us that our young people have comments to make on religion today to which we may well listen. We should not forget that a large number of them have actually passed through the valley of the shadow and have emerged less squeamish about many of its details than we. This generation has explored some of the lowest depths of tragedy and in consequence has asked questions of a very searching nature. We can take courage, I think, from the fact that its own answers are so rarely of a morbid or unduly pessimistic sort. After all, we should not surrender either to the skeptical existentialists or to the relativistic and on the whole non-rational Freudians the exclusive right to the treatment of the topics of pain and death. Heidegger with his idea that life is carried on with death in view and that death in setting limits to life is a great individualizing factor, marking off the domain that is ours and ours alone, has helped to restore death as a proper object for philosophizing. But the discussion of care, anxiety, and guilt to which he is led has its morbid overtones. Youth does not accept them and neither should we. Pain and death must be brought out into the open as topics for reflection. The next step is to treat them with the perceptiveness that refuses to consider them final.

At this point, however, we are assailed by doubts. The problem of evil is, after all, the rock on which many a theological system has foundered. Do we really think that where so many others have come to grief we shall be able to avoid disaster? The only answer is that the efforts to deal with this problem have not all been failures and that by reviewing some of them we may at least see the direction from which the solution must come. Let us turn first to the great teacher of India. Buddha and this problem are closely linked in our minds. No other leader of history has saturated his teaching more completely with the idea that suffering is always and everywhere with us. Birth is suffering, he taught, and so is death; so also is the craving existence we call life which always wants what it does not get and gets what it does not want. But with all his greatness as a moral figure and in spite of the tremendous appeal of his compassionate personality I think we must agree that intellectually Buddha is more successful in posing the problem than in giving the answer. Since desire and dissatisfaction are coterminous, he taught, what we must do is to eliminate desire. In line with this negative doctrine one feels throughout his teaching an almost morbid shrinking from pain and a lack of the willingness to accept life and make the best of it which to us seems so necessary.

It is noteworthy, however, that Buddha's failure as a theorist is largely forgotten because of his great success as a man of action. His deeds belied his words, for after receiving the vision and adopting the idea that desire must be extinguished he went on to forty years of active preaching and organizing which involved the cultivation of a great number of desires. His example, that is, was better than his logic. Moved by the compassion so characteristic of all he did and with a sublime disregard for such a hobgoblin as consistency he helped others to overcome their desires at the cost of cultivating his own. The illustration is helpful because many besides Buddha have done the same. Unable to face the issue intellectually they quite rightly refuse to collapse before it and insist that the problem must be met in a practical way.

In our teaching we should, however, try to offer hints at a solution even though we have to admit that the complete outline is not within our grasp. I should like to turn for help at this point to three authors whose work seems to me especially significant. The first is Arthur Clutton Brock, distinguished literary critic of the London *Times*. In an essay called "The Visionaries" written in 1920 shortly before his death,

Clutton Brock speaks of Christ's belief that "behind the huge menacing universe of things" there was a "God who would not let a sparrow fall to the ground without being himself with it and of it." This, Clutton Brock goes on to say, represents

an absurd desperate affirmation, contrary to every item of our routine experience. An affirmation that provokes us, even while it allures; for, if it were true, why do we always live as if it were not? Why are we, after millions of years of human effort, having risen from flint implements to aeroplanes, after miracles of human skill and wisdom, utterly unconvinced of its truth, so that we still live in the routine world and have our investments, our armaments and our whole system of defences against nature and each other? Why do we go mad and suffer tortures and torture each other? This God must either be a figment or an absurd futile being, a contradiction in terms.

I am not attempting satire. I am weary of it and of all denunciations of the human race. I write in a mood of weariness, and I cannot believe, I am even distressed by the words "Come unto me all ye that labour and are heavy laden." They are printed words to me, repeated by men who know no more than I do. I do not see this God anywhere, and, though I might wish to believe in him so that I might have rest in illusion, I cannot.

Then the author draws a row of asterisks across the page. The next paragraph begins with the sentence: "But I cannot leave the matter thus."

To me this is a most dramatic representation of the central human quandary and our sole means of escape. We face the fact of human suffering and are overwhelmed. It shatters our confidence, breaks down our faith, leaves us feeling that our only hope is in illusion and thus undermines our belief in reason itself. Yet, at the lowest point of despair, we feel impelled to draw a row of asterisks across the page and to say: "But I cannot leave the matter thus." Why can't we leave it

thus? Simply, it seems to me, because life itself forces us to
go on. Life moves forward and we have to move with it.
Then, Clutton Brock hints, as we go forward we are faced
with practical decisions. These in turn must be made on the
basis of what we believe to be good and bad, and judgments
of good and evil, when we examine them, point to the right
of the good to demand our loyalty. And if the good requires
our loyalty it is itself of the nature of the divine and a world
which contains it must have a divine quality. This is not
Clutton Brock's phrasing but it is the substance of his thought.
When we face squarely the fact of pain we are forced practically to make decisions and to take active steps which have
extremely important implications for theory.

The insight of William James, the second author I wish to
discuss, was similar. It is true that James has a great deal to
say about supernatural help and that often he talks about
salvation from sin. But one who studies him carefully can see
that what really concerned him was the universal undeserved
suffering of mankind and the attitude one should take toward
it. In spite of the optimism we associate with his eloquent
descriptions of the will to survive, to achieve, and to believe,
pessimism of a very dark sort was for James a real alternative.
Frequently he affirms that it ranges through the deeper levels
of experience where happiness and good cheer are out of
place. Expressed in a sentence, his answer to the problem
was that we must meet suffering with courage and that in
refusing to allow pain to dictate to us we imply a belief both
in the worth-whileness of the struggle and in the essential
goodness or godlike quality of a universe which demands that
courage be displayed.

The issue comes out clearly in his essay on "The Sentiment
of Rationality," where he twits Herbert Spencer and his
disciples with a lack of logic. It is impossible for Spencer to
maintain, James says, that the inner heart of the universe is

unknowable and at the same time to affirm that we should live with energy though energy bring pain. For if the latter be true the former cannot be. If we say that it is necessary to live with energy, though energy bring pain, we are saying something not merely about ourselves and our resolves but about a world in which such resolution and action are called for. The universe, then, is not ultimately mysterious but is the kind that lays upon us moral demands that we recognize as valid.

"We have seen our buddy and our enemy die," said the returned veteran, "and we have become compassionate." Our need to go on not merely with courage but also with compassion is brought out still more plainly by the third author I wish to quote—our great contemporary Albert Schweitzer. Any reader of his autobiography quickly becomes aware of Schweitzer's sensitiveness to pain in other beings, animal as well as human. In his feeling for the unity of the entire sentient world Schweitzer is almost a Buddhist. Buddhistic also is his disillusionment over life's hopes. Consider this passage from his *Civilization and Ethics* (Eng. tr. p. 209):

Life attracts us with a thousand expectations and fulfills hardly one of them. And the fulfilled expectation is almost a disappointment, for only anticipated pleasure is really pleasure; in pleasure which is fulfilled its opposite is already stirring. Unrest, disappointment, and pain are our lot in the short span of time which lies between our entrance on life and our departure from it. The spiritual is in a dreadful state of dependence on our bodily nature. Our existence is at the mercy of meaningless happenings and can be brought to an end by them at any moment. The will-to-live gives me an impulse to action, but the action is just as if I wanted to plow the sea, and sow in the furrows. What did those who worked before me effect? What significance in the endless chain of world-happenings have their efforts had? With all its illusive promises the will-to-live only means to mislead me into prolonging my existence, and allowing to enter on existence other beings to whom the same miserable lot has been assigned as to myself so that the game may go on and on without end.

Schweitzer's efforts to wrestle with the problem are especially illuminating because he is so explicit in his idea that the solution must be intellectual as well as practical. Over and over again he counsels us to use our minds, to refuse to yield to the emotional suggestibility of the moment, to look back on the age of reason as a great creative period in history, and to be confident that in the end we shall be able to think our way through our problems. When he finally comes to the crux of the matter he presents us with a peculiar fact. His answer is not strictly a rationalistic answer yet it certainly cannot be called irrational. It is as though the head had been forced to yield to the demands of the heart and the practical will but had insisted that it do so on its own terms.

External nature, Schweitzer says, is an enigma. We cannot find in it the evidence of one increasing purpose for which we yearn. In this sense the mind is flouted in its attempt to prove the existence of God. But if we turn to the inner life and probe our deepest emotions we discover a driving will to live which we know we share with all other sentient beings. Schweitzer's way of treating this discovery is peculiarly significant. "I am life that wills to live," he says, "in the midst of other life that wills to live." Reverence for life thus becomes the supreme ethical formula. Why? we ask. Is there anything moral about life itself? Cannot life be grasping and selfish as well as compassionate? Did not Nietzsche also look within himself for the will to live only to find that it was a symbol of the will to power and of the ruthless competitive drive that will brook no interference? The clue to the difference is, I think, that Schweitzer in testing his emotions made use of an *intellectual* criterion that Nietzsche missed. It is only *consistent*, Schweitzer says in effect, to measure my desires by those *of others* and to fit them into the larger pattern others form. They cannot be judged in isolation. They are data to be accepted and placed along with further data in a coherent and harmonious pattern. As we explore the recesses of the heart, that is to say, we must not forget the lessons that the head has taught us. The mind strives always to take account of the total picture and to keep its parts in their proper relation. Rightly understood, our sympathies do the same. Although he does not put the matter in just these terms Schweitzer thus seems to me to offer a striking instance of the common purpose shared by head and heart and of the fact that at this crucial point where they appear to part company actually their methods are the same. It is another bit of evidence that even where our deepest feelings are concerned the appeal to the irrational is out of court.

At the risk of sheer sentimental dalliance over an issue in which our emotions are deeply involved we have lingered with this question of suffering. Our conclusion must be that the time is ripe for a new attack which will view it as a point not of arrest but of departure. If we seek a place where thought, feeling, and act fuse we seem to have found it here. But if we use it for a new beginning we must face the need for a change in our thought about God. The theology which emphasizes sin emphasizes also an omnipotent God whose authority stems from his power as Creator. The fact of undeserved pain has always raised questions about such a God. Today theological theory insists with a new emphasis that the God of creation be given his rightful due while actual experience reveals more suffering than ever before and more doubts about a God who permits it.

Must we not say that these doubts point in the right direction? In his *Dialogues Concerning Natural Religion* Hume makes Cleanthes observe: "I scruple not to allow that I have been apt to suspect the frequent repetition of the word *infinite*, which we meet with in all theological writers, to savour more of panegyric than of philosophy, and that any purpose of reasoning, and even of religion, would be better served were we to rest contented with more accurate and more moderate expressions." Mill expressed the same skepticism, we recall, and in our own day Professor E. S. Brightman has eloquently and convincingly explained how God can be "finite" and yet the object of our religious devotion. Whitehead and, following him, Hartshorne have suggested that there is a sense in which God as relative, unstable, and growing is a richer conception than God as absolute and unchanging. The potential element in God's nature makes compassion possible for Him. Furthermore, it is our nature as individuals not to be completely determined by an omnipotent Power. Even the ancients were less susceptible to the lure of omnipotence as an idea than we sometimes think. Boodin has shown that the Genesis story is not concerned with creation *ex nihilo* but with transformation from chaos to order, and that the God it describes is like Plato's in the *Timaeus* who imposes measure and number on a world lacking both. The great ethical prophets implied agreement with this view since evil was regarded by them as something for which God could not be held responsible.

It was Augustine who stressed omnipotence because he felt that the incarnation could take place only if matter were not wholly evil, so that God must be responsible for matter as for all else. And it is to Augustinianism that our neo-orthodox have appealed in their effort to restore the faith of our fathers. As I have said before, I think the appeal is dangerous. Theoretically it makes the problem of evil insoluble. Practically it will tend in the future as it has in the past to exalt not merely God but his representatives on earth—or those who claim to be—as arbiters of good and evil, life and death. In a day when we have learned to be on the alert for tyranny in all its forms we should not miss it when it dogs the footsteps of theology. A God whose authority rests ultimately on his power over us is actually no God for us to worship. We fear power and obey it if we must, but the motive of our obedience is not loving devotion.

But if God be the force of love discovered in the upward thrust of our common life whose influence we feel especially as we face the fact of pain, then, although we do not know all the answers, we know enough to give us a basis for practical faith. Love must suffer long, seeking not its own or any sectarian end. Love must disclose itself as a quality which is not imposed on human life by any authoritarian or sovereign will but which grows out of our awareness of our common need. Faith must show that love has its roots in the demands laid on us in our common humanity and that it develops in the struggling growth toward the light which we share with our fellow-men. The Greek sculptors and philosophers were right when they took their ideal standards from the dynamic symmetry which the growing body has in common with all living things, not from the abstractions of geometry nor yet from the stunted perversions suggested by original sin.

Faith in a growing God of love gives us a basis for action. It offers us also a way of meeting our scientific friends on their own terms instead of flouting their research by the appeal to a special revelation. For modern science refuses to try to answer the question how the world began. Speculations as to the origin of energy and motion can be guesses and nothing more. But within the whirlpool of crosscurrents that we call our universe are evidences of one type of change that scientists themselves agree is change with direction. It marks the transition from the simple to the complex and, as Gerald Heard adds in his Ayer Lectures, from the diffused to the defined. We are on sure ground if we cling to the fact of this development from star dust to conscious life as one trend in this extraordinary world—not the only one, but the one which to us is far and away the most important. Of it we are a part. We are its creation in the only sense in which the word has religious significance. But to it loyalty is owed not because it has produced us and not simply because it has creative power but because the love we believe it shares with us is the highest spiritual quality we know. Faith of this sort not only meets the demands of our hearts but goes on to require that our minds be stretched to their limits to understand what it implies.

V. The Ministry of Art

WHY have we failed to develop the richness of experience that religious insight requires? To this question our thought continually returns. In the last lecture we saw that there is much to be done on the problem of pain and that quite possibly we may be able to deal with it in such a way as to develop more constructive religious perceptiveness than we have had before. But there are other types of awareness we have hardly tapped. Our brief contact with Isaiah showed us that the experience of mystery may itself be made a datum for religious experience. In some respects we seem to know more today about both pain and mystery than did our fathers. Should our experience not make us more sensitive? If we think of God as the claim laid upon us by the universe that we do our jobs faithfully, should we not know more about God than men have known before? Was any other generation given so much data for both knowledge and feeling as ours and such a chance to discover what the claim itself means?

As we ponder this question our thought can hardly help turning toward that phase of experience in which men have sought to communicate what in so many of its aspects must remain incommunicable. Through art some of the most gifted minds of the race have found a way of responding to the beauty, the agony, the mystery, and the feeling of kinship presented by the world around them. If we are interested in a rational faith should we not examine the metaphysical demand that hovers in the background of the artist's work? Have we paid enough attention to art as the handmaid of religion? If faith is actually the fulfillment and not the denial of our rational and cultural life, it would seem that art, properly understood, should provide a type of experience needed for the religious interpretation of the world.

From one point of view the final judgment on this problem of the relation of religion to art is set forth in the illustration from Hosea's experience cited earlier. Hosea was artist, prophet, and religious reformer all in one. He was an artist first of all in the fact that in order to solve his problems he withdrew into the world of his private feeling and found there a solution which itself was not private. Hosea answers the old question as to whether the artist seeks only individual self-expression or strives to communicate with others by showing that when the problem is itself a significant one much more than sheer individual feeling is involved. If his experience is a criterion, the artist has not merely an overpowering impulse to withdraw from others but just as strong an urge to return with a message that can be shared. We recall that in Hosea's case private grief and disillusionment led to the discovery of what the common lot of man is and to the further discovery of what must be done to ameliorate it. The individual experience became an instance of the universal and the universal itself became a stimulus to action.

It is interesting to speculate at what point Hosea stopped being an artist and became a prophet. Certainly the call to action appears to have little to do with the artist's inspiration, yet a life dedicated wholly to contemplation with no concern for getting anything done would seem truncated and unfinished even from the artist's point of view. This lecture will raise the question whether the return to action so characteristic of the mystic is not foreshadowed in the life of the artist, and also whether religion and art do not overlap at many more points than Kierkegaardian neo-orthodoxy is willing to admit. "True artists," said Rodin, "are the most religious of mortals." This is an extravagant statement, but in its enthusiasm it points to the vividly religious quality that sensitive observers have always found in great art.

We saw in the last lecture that we may not flinch before the fact of evil and that if we face it squarely it can lift us up out of ourselves to the level of the shared purpose. But do we reflect often enough on the need for facing squarely the fact of good? And have we done all we should to bring home to ourselves the sheer goodness art presents and its dependence on the strongly felt distinction between good and bad? That our aesthetic preferences depend on taste is true. But do we really believe that there is no disputing about tastes and that our preferences here have nothing to do with what is preferred by reason and conscience? In other words, has religion done what it could to cultivate goodness for *all* that it is worth?

The presence of value in this universe of physical electrons as a datum which challenges reason, conscience, and taste is certainly the religious fact *par excellence*. It is by discovering why value is here and what it means that we shall find God if we find him at all. In the traditional triad of truth, goodness, and beauty the last-named has unquestionably been hardest for theology to deal with. Truth's claims we recognize whenever we attempt rational thought. Goodness we admire and expect to find in others if not in ourselves. But beauty is different. It seems to belong to the more relaxing experiences and to be less a stimulus than a luxury. Beauty, says Somerset Maugham, brings us to a full stop. Perhaps Kierkegaard was right, then, when he accused it of irresponsibility. Keats has said that beauty is truth, and Boileau that nothing is beautiful but the truth, yet we have felt that this is prejudiced counsel. A book has appeared called *The Moral Obligation to Be Intelligent* but we have yet to see a modern study of the moral need to have beauty or to be aware of it. Indeed, many a critic reminds us that when morals come in by the door art flies out through the window, so that if they occupy the same room at all it is through convenience and not love. Typical of most opinion is an essay headed "Art as an Antidote to Morality."

Art brings its own mood. Not only is it a fleeting one but it occupies its own exclusive sphere, making no claims on either belief or action—such at least is the common view. Art is then, to use the popular word, an escape, or if it is anything more, this moreness brings merely increased subjectivity and, in the case of much modern art, increased subjectivity of a dissatisfied and even hypochondriacal sort. The world, say these moderns, is not only too much with us but is with us in a completely unbearable way. Leave us, then, with our traumas, our fantasies, our insufficiently sublimated libidos, and our overpowering complexes, or at most give us the relief that comes from telling you that we have them.

Yet the unfinished character of this sort of description of art's aims is apparent. "There is no surer way of evading the world than through art," said Goethe, but he went on to say: "and there is no surer way of binding oneself to it than through art." What he seems to have meant is that there is a kind of polarity in artistic experience whereby the artist first sets up a barrier to separate himself from the outside world and then breaks it down by the creative genius with which he approaches reality to rebuild it. Retreat into inner privacy is necessary. The Kierkegaardians have shown its importance in religion; the moderns exemplify it in art. This, however, is but one stage. Kierkegaard takes the next step by means of a miracle. But great art allows for the unfolding of a natural emotional experience. At the start it throws us in upon ourselves. But then it takes us out of ourselves, first by introducing us to the realm of form as an intrinsic quality with its own recognizable worth, second by inducing moods that struggle to communicate, and third by revealing the rhythmic current of passive feeling and active will. It is this which enables us not only to reconcile the inner world of feeling with the outer world of fact but to transform fact so that at least in some small degree it is brought into line with the heart's desire.

Art need not have the "demonic" or self-righteous connotation that some of our theologians ascribe to it. The artist who uses his inspiration to inflate his own ego has conspicuously missed his calling. Nor can the experience of the beautiful be leveled down to mere titillation or to the plane of sheer hedonism. Rigorist that he was, and unyielding in the belief that to be moral an act must be difficult, the great Immanuel Kant yet held art in high esteem and claimed that an experience which involved only sensuous stimulation was not aesthetic at all. True art, he said, is not accompanied by selfish pleasure. In this both Hegel and Lotze agreed. As far back as Plato and Plotinus philosophers have held that the Beautiful is not only significant morally but an object of actual religious adoration.

Indeed, one of the most fascinating threads in that extraordinary fabric we call the history of religions has to do with the continuous attempt to combine art and religion and to read into one the meaning of the other. According to Miss Jane Harrison, art and religious ritual sprang from a single primitive ceremony. The sequence was: first the hunt, then the ritualistic dance, and later the development of drama, sculpture, priests, gods, and theologies. In other words, first there was withdrawal into feeling, then the feeling was "bodied forth," as the saying goes, and used as a means of creating religious, aesthetic, and intellectual objects in the environment. The Greek struggle, only partly successful, to bring the varied religious objects under the control of one idea and to reconcile the pluralism of experience to the control of one God is well known. Religiously speaking, the Greeks didn't really have a word for it. But what they lacked here in clarity they did make up in richness, and so alert was their sense for the intangible that the line between religious and aesthetic elements is exceedingly hard to draw. One cannot name an art practiced in Greece which was not from beginning to end dedicated to the worship of the gods. Sir Charles Eliot in his monumental *Hinduism and Buddhism* is authority for a similar statement with regard to India. The records of the Nile show the same to be true for Egypt. We do not think of the Hebrews as particularly concerned with art, but they made the beautiful temple of Solomon the center of their religious life, and we have already seen that when their religious feeling reached its height, in the work of psalmists and prophets, it found expression in rhythmic, poetic utterance. Their cousins the Arabs did not show an inkling of aesthetic interest until they were fired by religious zeal.

It is interesting to note also that throughout history a change in either artistic or religious feeling seems to have been accompanied by a change in the other. When, for example, the coming of Zen forms of belief and practice diverted Japanese Buddhism into mystical channels, Japanese painting turned to landscapes and portraits with an emphasis in each case on mystical suggestion in place of realism. In seventeenth-century Europe when Pascal, George Herbert, and Milton were standing in religious awe before the mysterious silence of the infinite heavenly regions, baroque architecture was busy with the problems of space, Dutch landscape painters introduced what they called "atmospheric infinity" into their paintings, and Rembrandt was using chiaroscuro to hint at the changes that occur in light as it emerges from its mysterious cosmic background. Later, in the nineteenth century, as has been pointed out by Albrecht Ritschl, counterpoint, heroic poetry, and standardized architecture were matched in religion by a priori thought and the physicotheological argument for God. The coming of Rousseau and Goethe in literature, Delacroix and Millet in painting, Schumann and Schubert in music brought the kind of pietism and pantheism which the name Schleiermacher suggests in theology.

Now of course all this may mean simply that when people are in a certain frame of mind they look for a few set ways of expressing themselves whether their particular interest be art or religion. But the kinship is so close that it appears to represent something much more fundamental than a mere surface similarity. Both art and religion, we have said, first take us to the kingdom of ends, second struggle to communicate a truth that is not easily put into words, third present us with a sensitive awareness of the rhythm by which life swings from contemplation to action, from worship to work. Let us examine these common characteristics.

First of all, art and religion give us as clear instances as life affords of what it means to experience an end in itself. One feels sometimes as though the pragmatic philosophy would be justified, if on no other ground, for the negative illustration it offers of the same principle. Pragmatism, that is to say, with its emphasis on use helps us to see more clearly those areas of experience to which usefulness does not apply. Useful as justice may be, we value it not on that account but simply because as justice it has an intrinsically valuable quality that gives it a legitimate claim upon us. The same may be said of truth, of friendship, or of love. Certainly beauty falls into this classification also, and art which presents beauty to us makes its appeal to this side of our nature. If one asks how and why this is possible the nearest answer is that art presents us with formal, harmonious structure and that form as such has a claim on our emotions similar to that which reason with its own related and consistent pattern has on our minds. It is true, of course, that art often makes a directly sensuous appeal. The beautiful blue of a vase of the Ming dynasty speaks to our hearts immediately and establishes a bond between its creator and ourselves that will not be denied. But it is hard to think of a work of art as sheer color or sheer sound with no formal element, and it is to the fact of formal pattern that we finally turn when we try to analyze art's appeal.

Like religion, art brings unity and harmony out of diversity and chaos. It reconciles the warring elements in existence. It lifts us from the parts to a wholeness which encompasses and throws new light upon them. This, I think, is what Clive Bell had in mind when he said that a work of art is always haunted by the universal which informs every particular. The particulars hint at the universal, without which they would lose their particularity. Back of our partial meanings there is a whole, back of our frustrations there is fulfillment, back of our disorder there is the harmony of the consistent pattern. Art suggests this to us, never too obviously (especially at the present time!) but always hauntingly and always —in genuine art—persuasively. So it is that art gives us not merely the general reassurance that some things are to be preferred to others. It confronts us also with the particular value of form, wholeness, organization and, as was said above, does this for our feelings much as reason does it for our minds. It convinces us that some things ought to be, not only because they are right and better than other things but because their organization, their plan, their relationships, and their wholeness make them better. Of the great work of art as of reason or the moral ideal we say, "It had to be so."

The intrinsic quality in art comes out also as we notice the words we apply to works of art we admire. This one is "genuine," we say; it has "authenticity" or "integrity." Such words do not express a pragmatic judgment. They apply to a set of inner relationships which have nothing to do with utility or results.

In what respect does religion differ from the aesthetic experience described here? Must we not find the difference in the fact that it simply goes farther along the same line? The mystic sees unity, pattern, wholeness, but he is surer than the artist that it applies to the universe and he is less willing to confine it within the borders of a single impression. The mystic has not merely a succession of moods bringing a series of ends in themselves but an experience in which he believes he comes into touch with the final End, the God who must be worshiped for his own sake and for his inner intrinsic quality of value. This was the real insight of Hosea, and not his alone but that of Amos, Isaiah, and Micah. This was the final perception of Job as he matched Satan's sneering utilitarianism ("Doth Job fear God for naught?") with the vision of the intrinsic value revealed to him after his varied experiences of suffering, dialectic, humility before nature, and wonder at the Mind by which nature is overruled.

So it is that William Temple can say in *Mens Creatrix* "In the experience of such transcendent Beauty we realize the hope of mysticism. In a single impression we receive what absolutely satisfies us, and in that perfect satisfaction we are lost. Duration vanishes. The 'moment eternal' is come. The grand drama proceeds; the music surges through us; we are not conscious of our existence. We hear and see; and when all is done we consider and bow the head." More eloquently, perhaps, than anyone else in the history of literature

Plotinus pleads for awareness of the primal religious unity which is presupposed in rational argument, implied in the fragmentariness of our moral life, and revealed in beauty. "Until," says Plotinus, "passing on the upward way all that is other than God, each in the solitude of himself shall behold that solitary-dwelling Existence, the Apart, the Unmingled, the Pure, that from which all things depend, for which all look and live and act and know the Source of Life and of Intellection and of Being. . . . First let each become godlike and each beautiful who cares to see God and Beauty. . . . The primal Good and the primal Beauty have the one dwelling-place and thus always Beauty's seat is there."

Obviously both art and religion lead us to a kingdom of ends. What it is that they say about this kingdom is, however, not always easy to determine. The mystic has an experience that he himself calls ineffable and beyond all attempts at description. Yet he spends much of his life trying to communicate its meaning. The artist is apt to be touchy even on the subject of attempted communication. "Let me alone," he is inclined to say. "I am trying to express myself and that is enough. Whether the message gets across to others is no part of my responsibility and actually of little interest to me." Yet it seems impossible to leave the artist in his seclusion. If his work represents merely his private mood in its petulance we can really have no interest in it and it is hard to see how we can call it art. Only because it has something important to say to us has it a real claim on our attention. In fact, until comparatively recently art's ability to communicate seems to have been taken for granted. Gilson observes that for the great painters of the Middle Ages *to be* was itself the same thing as *to signify*. They looked on nature as revelation and thought of their job as that of making the revelation more clear. "What is called poetry," said Ramuz, much nearer our own time, whom Gilson quotes, "is the perception of the sacred. It is the need, after perceiving it, to make other men share in it . . . for indeed if the sacred is not everywhere, it is nowhere. And what does this mean, if not that all poetry is religious, that all poetry is a kind of religion?"

Our own doubts of art's ability to communicate are therefore another bit of evidence of the extreme subjectivity into which our age has fallen. Obviously art must not be too realistic, too photographic, or too representational. It is also true that the unity and the wholeness must not be too stark but must be hinted at with suggestiveness and sublety. Yet obscurity in itself is never a virtue. Indeed, it begins to appear that it was never less a virtue than now, when the times cry out for a great idea that people can understand and share. We cannot permit the rise of a new pseudo-aristocracy in these matters of taste. The influence of modern art will become actually pernicious if we allow its retreat into the trivial and ironic, the fanciful and the distorted, to make us feel that its message is esoteric, unavailable to the common man, and therefore out of place in a democracy.

This leads us to our third question, which has to do with the way both religion and art reveal the rhythm of contemplation and action, worship and work. As all writers on the subject show, the paradox of mysticism is that what is sought as an end in itself does not remain isolated or irrelevant but finds its appropriate place in the dynamic flow of experience. The pendulum swings from work to worship but it also swings back again. God is worshipped for his own sake, yet in the highest sense he proves to be of use in the moral struggle. Art has been less successful in expressing the return movement to the world of action but, as in the question whether art communicates, so here we are bound to see that an art completely remote from the world of affairs would have no interest for us at all. After all, art, as we so often have been told, is the re-creation of experience. Its own vision of goodness cannot help influencing our perceptions of goodness in other fields. We respond almost automatically to what is well done, or well presented, and to the essential rightness of an authoritative vision. True approval is active as well as passive. Our conduct cannot help being affected by the range and depth of what we admire. Why should we limit the "integrity" which we speak of in connection with great art to the formal pattern of a mood? Is not life itself, like music, a gradually unfolding pattern? And does not its own rhythm require that inner vision and outer act achieve final harmony?

One of the most eloquent descriptions of art as based on the presence of alternation in nature and in life is that of Professor John Dewey in his *Art as Experience*. Since the time when God promised Noah that seedtime and harvest, cold and heat, summer and winter, day and night should not cease, the rhythms of nature, Dewey holds, have vitally affected human doings and undergoings. Men carried their feeling for nature's periodicity into the rites which preceded and followed war, the chase, birth, and death. "Underneath the rhythms of each art," says Dewey, "as a substratum in the depths of the subconscious, is the basic pattern of the relations of the live creature to his environment." When men achieved greater control over their surroundings they carried the idea of rhythm into their more imaginative artistic projections, developing in pattern and design the alternations of action and reflection, of tension and repose, of surrender and release. And as art developed it became apparent that there is also a rhythmic alternation between the productive mood of the artist and the creative appreciation of the observer. Further, as Cassirer has pointed out, "symbolic forms" take their place in the observer's mind, helping him to organize his world and to understand its aesthetic quality. The observer feels tension between himself and his environment and then release as the formal pattern brings order, reconciliation, and understanding.

In religion the dramatic power of experiences which successively offer tension and release is brought home to us in the act of worship. Why, for example, are we stirred so deeply by a service in a Gothic cathedral? Is it not because the architecture itself, with its thin piers, narrow pointed windows, ribbed ceilings, and flying buttresses, brings a sense of strain which is relieved only as we think of the higher point at which these ascending lines aim and in which they finally meet? In its own way the plain song with its freedom from fixed meter and from the rules of harmony or counterpoint portrays the spontaneous rise and fall of human emotion, while the mass is of course a powerful representation of the rhythm of suffering, death, and spiritual triumph. The chief difficulty for us who believe in free and nonauthoritarian religion is that we are apt to associate this experience with services in the Roman Catholic Church where so frequently architecture, music, and ideas all point to the thirteenth century. The thirteenth was indeed a magnificent century, but alas, it is not the one in which we live. By contrast, a Protestant service in, say, an English cathedral retains the aura of tradition without the discordant note of the exotic and foreign. The culture of which it speaks is ours, as is the language, and the corporate experience is one in which we have participated and can understand. From our point of view it represents an advance upon the Middle Ages, for the worshiper has himself become a priest, authority has given way to freedom of interpretation, and counterpoint and harmony have called upon reasoned pattern to control the vagaries of human desire. The rhythm is that of thought and feeling instead of feeling alone. Art, philosophy, and religion have found common ground.

On the practical side the moral for the conduct of our own

services of worship is plain. Our architecture can be devotional whether we use Gothic to express the upward-thrusting energy which seeks for the God above or Georgian to represent the return movement of the divine as it tabernacles with men. Our music need not be of the stringy saccharine variety that our choirs so often prefer but should in its own way describe the resolution of variety in a final harmony. Perhaps it is ungracious to suggest that the sermon contributes the element of struggle, yet in a larger than personal sense this is true. The return to the discursive intellect must mean the return to the realm of debate. But if the sermon is really based on a great idea and is expressed with honesty, controversy will yield to assent and those who listen will find themselves bound together in the exaltation of the shared experience.

What, then, is the real difference between art and religion? Our claim throughout has been that religion brings art to completion in the sense that where art gives us a mood, an episode, or an isolated instance, religion takes into account the fullness of life. Art is concerned with the pattern of a particular moment, religion with the form that undergirds the universe and includes the individual experience. Our contention has also been that the line of demarcation is often difficult to draw and that when it is drawn so sharply as it seems to be by many in our modern age the result shows the artificiality of the line itself. Art cannot be private, uncommunicative, or indifferent to conduct without becoming insignificant and uninteresting. We began this chapter by using Hosea as an illustration and asking when he stopped being an artist and became a prophet. Before we close let us ask a similar question of the great composer Johann Sebastian Bach, the two-hundredth anniversary of whose death the year 1950 commemorates.

Was Bach a religious composer? Yes, of that there can

be no question. Would his art have been as great if it had lacked the religious overtones? Or is its religious quality an essential part of its power? Schweitzer calls Bach "the greatest of preachers." "What speaks through his work," Schweitzer affirms, "is pure religious emotion." This, he explains, is "emotion of the infinite and exalted for which words are always an inadequate expression." Bach's own testimony to his personal religious aim is just as emphatic. We are familiar with the headings he gave his music such as *"Soli Deo Gloria"* or *"Jesus juva."* On the title page of the *Klavierbüchlein* he wrote, *"In Nomine Jesu,"* and on the *Orgelbüchlein,* "For the glory of the most high God and for the instruction of my neighbor." "Like all other music," he once said, "the figured bass should have no other end and aim than the glory of God and the recreation of the soul." It is small wonder that Schweitzer remarks that for Bach music was an act of worship.

But what was its specifically religious quality? At first we are inclined to say that Bach is a religious composer because he takes us into the realm of pure form, because his music is so architectonic, and because he so obviously conveys to us the sense of that which through its intrinsic quality lays its demands on us. All great art should do this but Bach's work seems to be suffused with a special quality which makes the religious connotation inescapable. Where is it to be found? The answer we would suggest—a partial one at best,—is that Bach's life and his music point to a peculiar mastery of the rhythmic pattern of contemplation and action which in religion is so clear and which art fumbles for and has difficulty in expressing. First of all, as Schweitzer himself points out, Bach's own experience testifies to inner serenity accompanied by outward struggle. Some of his most haunting melodies appeal to death. They reveal his own inner communion with the spirit of death and his longing for relief from life's battle. Yet how clear is the fact of constant return. As a person Bach was virile, robust, and actively involved in meeting the demands of everyday existence. As a composer he was probably more productive than any other in history.

In the second place, although it is true that Bach takes us into the realm of pure form and shows himself to be a master of what has been called "absolute" music, it is just as true that he follows the pendulum as it swings to the other pole of controversy and writes music that is almost shamelessly "programmatic" in its representational quality and its direct appeal to the immediacy of the emotions of daily life. Resolute faith is represented by strong steps in the bass, lassitude by rhythmic uncertainty, Satan by a serpentine movement, Adam's fall by falling sevenths, angels ascending by joyous climbing scales. Clouds, water, trees, animals all have their musical counterparts.

In the third place, Bach seems deliberately to try to meet the criticism of aloofness and to prepare the way for an active emotional and moral response by his use of the chorale. As is well known, many of his chorales had their origin in the folk songs of the people and expressed less the formal criticism of the artist than the immediate feelings of the common man. In his oratorios Bach appears to make an extra effort to use this quality by assigning them to be sung not by soloists or chorus but by the congregation itself. The result is that while the people on the stage use the Biblical narrative to present the objective historical fact, the congregation makes its own subjective response. On the stage or in the choir loft and chancel is the datum of history. In the pews this datum is transformed and made part of the daily life of decision and action. This relevance of Bach's work to the practical task is not easy to describe, but the sensitive listener cannot miss it. One may compare Bach's treatment of the theme of redemption in his *St. Matthew Passion* with the way Wagner deals with a similar theme in *Parsifal*. Wagner's is clearly a stage play or a spectacle, based on a medieval legend, appealing to an atmosphere of the supernatural and using music that, with all its beauty, is so highly romanticized as to fail in freeing itself from its inner turmoil. The opera as a whole is impressionistic, appealing to a mood, and remaining finally oblivious to the questions: Is this true? and What should we do? In Bach's work these two issues are met. The Passion story lays claim to truth and inspires to action. It comes from the Bible and is based on historical fact. Its setting is that not of the theater but of the church. And the music appeals to those elemental rhythms which speak to us of what is fundamental both in nature and in the religious life of man. "I express it to myself," said Goethe after listening to Bach, "as if the eternal harmony were communing with itself as might have happened in God's bosom shortly before the creation of the world."

A word should be added on a problem which grows out of the foregoing and which has its own perplexities. If art is so close to religion why is the artist likely to profess indifference to the moral struggle which is one of religion's chief concerns? If the vision of what is right and good is so compelling to the artist's eye in his own field, why is he often so blind in the field of social relations? No one seems to have a satisfactory answer to this question. Tolstoy, it is true, spent much of his life trying to show the close connection of art and morals. Santayana has said that the aesthetic and moral judgments are closer to each other than either is to the intellectual judgment. And Henry Sturt has gone so far as to tell us that "Moral goodness, intellectual power, high vitality and strength are conditions and consequences of an artistic disposition." But in spite of these and countless other quotable statements the personal example too often presented is that of a great artist who is petty as a man.

The reason seems to be that the artist is too completely

immersed in one type of effort to be able to pay attention to other types. As primarily a perceiver of sensuous material he has had to limit himself to a special field and in so doing has cut himself off from the larger view. Charles A. Bennett has said that we start as lovers of beauty but end as hedonists. As a principle for the ordering of life, beauty, he says, has not enough vigor to confront and assimilate its opposite. It allows us to rest content with syntheses that are premature. Yet one feels that art is constantly reaching for the larger synthesis even when it fails to attain it. Leo Stein once wrote: "My ideal of a picture is that every part of it should oblige the looker-on who has any real sense for the whole to see the rest." Why should art be content with a whole that is only a part?

Here again Kierkegaard saw the problem but not the answer. We give art its due not by strengthening its sense for its own self-imposed limitations but by encouraging it to come out from under them. If religion can be so certain that faith without works is dead, and that contemplation must result in action, art can also recover a sense of its responsibilities. The picture, play, or symphony induces a mood but the mood can hardly exist as part of the stream of experience without making a claim both on our beliefs as to what is true and on our decisions as to what should be done. If the mood is a good one, or even if it is bad, it cannot be cut off from other moods. Goodness in one area reaches out for goodness elsewhere just as the privacy of the artist struggles for expression and through expression for communication. Indeed, our dissatisfaction with modern art comes in large part from the fact that so often it seems shut off by itself in angry defiance. Ours is truly an age of morbid introspection but morbid introspection cannot produce greatness in either art or theology. So long as we continue to stress to ourselves what we call the predicament of modern man and to emphasize his frailty and folly it is hard to see how we can deserve any art except the kind which presents us with the distortions of futility.

Man is indeed in a predicament; but he can face it with dignity. Though he has failed at certain crucial points in his moral development he has not lost his own integrity. What we need today is an art that in its own subtle way will express our confidence that even now decency, courage, and love can win the battle. The makings of a spiritual crusade are here. The resources of the world of unseen reality wait to be used by the artist who is also a consecrated man. Let us be careful, therefore, about encouraging this retreat into inarticulate privacy, realizing that we have a common problem and that we need the artist's help if we are to solve it. But let art once more become the handmaid of religion, finding in the manifold fruits of the spirit the object of its interest, and the first move will be made toward binding up the wounds of our modern life.

VI. Withdrawal and Return

READERS of Arnold Toynbee's popular book *A Study of History* have noticed his skillful use of the figure of "withdrawal and return." According to Toynbee, history has sometimes moved forward by the withdrawal of a great individual to a period of lonely meditation followed by his return equipped with a new set of rules for social behavior. Or a nation may itself withdraw, as did England from Continental affairs after the defeat of the Spanish Armada, in order to work out a theory of parliamentary government. Others than Toynbee have developed similar ideas of the ebb and flow of the tides of social and personal life, notably commentators like Professor Delacroix and Professor Hocking, who have shown the rhythmic succession of contemplation and action in the experience of the mystic.

The figure is useful for a discussion of reasonable religion because reason, like religion, has its alternating periods of withdrawal and return, and a religion which tries to be reasonable must take special account of them. It seems certain, also, that the opposition to religion of this type stems in large part from a misunderstanding of what "return" in this connection can mean. Indeed, the word "return" itself is ambiguous and unsatisfactory because it suggests that facts are faced and feelings indulged only *after* withdrawal has occurred. The truth is, of course, that the process of alternation is continuous. The mystic, for example, must prepare for his period of contemplation by strenuous moral discipline; the man of reason must seek data to submit to his processes of analysis and discrimination. Nor should we allow the word "reason" to stand in our minds only for the more passive aspect of our mental life. It has an aggressive activity of its own. In the ordinary pursuit of knowledge we use the experience of the senses to search for data which we can bring before the bar of judgment and in addition we use our emotions as instruments of perception. In religion the role of the emotions is much more prominent. The data for our faith in God come from our experiences of value and our beliefs as to what they tell us about our world. A religion of reason is thus in truth a religion of deep emotion and should be so understood.

Says T. S. Eliot:

> There is a time for building
> And a time for living and for generation
> And a time for the wind to break the loosened pane. . . .[1]

William James was concerned with the same problem when he asked: "Who can decide offhand which is obviously better —to live or to understand life?" "We must do both alternately," he answered, "and a man can no more limit himself to either than a pair of scissors can cut with a single one of its blades." "Thinking and doing, doing and thinking—that," says Goethe, "is the sum of all wisdom, recognized and practiced from of old, yet not understood by everyone. Like breathing in and out, both should occupy life in a ceaseless alternating flux; like question and answer, neither should occur without the support of the other."

The figure of withdrawal and return is also useful for our

---

[1] "East Coker" in *Four Quartets*. Copyright, 1943, by Harcourt, Brace & Co. and reprinted by permission.

discussion because it suggests that the dualism or doubleness of life is not that of two irreconcilable opposites. Bitter as is our experience of suffering, we do not seem to be justified in thinking of God as opposed by a devil or as frustrated by man's original sin. Tragedy results not from evil that is ineradicable but from our failure to do what we should. There seems no reason to believe that the failure was inevitable or that it cannot progressively be made less. God as the Rational Good confronts the world, which is neither rational nor good but has possibilities of becoming both. Within ourselves we find not so much a hereditary tendency toward sin as a set of driving impulses closely connected with the instincts of the body which in themselves are amoral and may be developed along either good or bad lines. Set over against these are the various influences experience brings us of a whole-making or reasonable sort which try to keep each desire from being too individualistic and to assign it an appropriate place in the larger pattern. Withdrawal, whether for rational synthesis or religious contemplation, is one of the ways of bringing this larger, whole-making influence into play. The familiar contrast of nature and reason or romantic impulse and classical form helps us to see what is involved. The greatest works of art are concerned with the struggle and reconciliation this contrast provokes. The most satisfactory religion should be the one which makes it most vivid. But we should be clear that it is really a *contrast* with which we have to do and not a contradiction.

In our first lecture we turned to the college campus for illustrations of our religious problem and possible ways of facing it. Let us now visit the campus once more in the effort to see what a religion that is rational must do to make itself practical. Colleges are conspicuous for their readiness to withdraw and for the difficulty they have in accomplishing the process of return. If we can see what the college does to make ideas effective in practical life, and more particularly what it fails to do, we may be helped to see the pitfalls that lie before a rational religion and the ways of avoiding them.

To begin with, college teaching sometimes tries to isolate ideas from feelings and from personal attitudes in an arbitrary way. Often this results from an unwillingness to face the fact that the give-and-take between feelings and ideas is constant. We sometimes say in college that we will teach the facts and that our concern is not with attitudes as such. But we should remember that attitudes of one sort or another are what our students are learning from us, whether we like it or not. If through laziness or indecision we refuse to teach our convictions, others with more energy or fewer scruples will do the teaching for us and the results will be the opposite of what we want. We should remember also the extent to which attitudes influence our learning of facts. If the student has curiosity he will absorb the facts that satisfy it. If he has honesty he will arrange them with integrity. If he has loyalty and love he will see their social implications. All these examples of the way our feelings work should help us to see that a religion dedicated to reason can never really be aloof. Our emotions and will are always at work and the task of seeing that they work in the right way is always with us.

In the next place, a charge often leveled against our college teaching is that in becoming analytical and detailed it has lost the larger point of view. In the days of the Olympians of fifty years ago, for example, men turned to philosophy for light on the problem of how to live. Today philosophy is immersed in certain specialized problems of logic. The men teaching it are as large minded and as humane as their predecessors. But philosophy as a subject is so bogged down in technicalities that the teacher who wants to use the broader approach literally does not know where to begin. Here again the man of rational faith must be on his guard against the idea that to be reasonable is to make more use of analysis than of synthesis. Worship has its own way of restoring the vision of the whole and it must not be neglected.

Thirdly, the man who pins his faith to reason should take account of a special occupational disease that often works havoc in a college community. There appears to be something about the process of mastering a difficult intellectual problem which brings to both teachers and students a feeling of complacency and of indifference not only to what is outside one's field but to one's own shortcomings in this field or any other. Notable exceptions at once spring to mind. The really great teacher, like the man who has really understood what reason requires, is free from pride as he is from most human faults. But it remains true that smugness is an insidious academic vice and is sometimes found where least expected. Surprisingly often proficiency in a special field of learning leads the scholar, like the artist, to a kind of contempt for what does not concern him and to an extremely provincial point of view. "Pride of intellect" is sin even though the phrase does not mean what the neo-orthodox think it does.

Finally, we should not forget that the popular criticism of philosophy, the colleges, and the life of reason in general has some basis. Unless it is constantly prodded philosophy does seek the armchair. Unless they are continually stimulated our colleges will pay more attention to withdrawal than they do to return. The campus itself emphasizes life's gracious amenities and tries to shut out any reference to its injustice and frustration. The result is that our frail human nature, glad of any pretext to avoid action, falls easily into the belief that it has solved a problem merely by talking about it. William James dealt with this situation in his famous essay on "A Moral Equivalent for War." If, as James suggested, our young people could be drafted for work in the mines, on the farms, and in the factories, and could use this experience to gather data about themselves and their society, they would have a much better understanding of what the intellectual life really means and what its responsibilities are. Again, what is true for the college student applies to the man who tries to work out a rational faith. He must constantly seek opportunities to explore the wider and deeper ranges of experience and must never allow himself to believe that to be reasonable is to be aloof.

The great teachers of the race have always known that the truth which is really understood and taken to heart is that which has become incarnate and has insisted on living on intimate terms with men. What is truth? asked jesting Pilate and waited not for an answer. But Pilate was a blind as well as jesting fool, for truth in its profoundest form stood before him as he spoke. What is virtue? asked Plato. In the Dialogues the answer emerges less as an abstract idea to be argued over than as a personal example of a brave man who was able to meet the temptations of the banquet, the skepticism of critics, and the imminence of death with resolution, patience, and courage. What is reality? asked the disciples of the Buddha. Over and over again their teacher replied that he could not tell them. But his forty years of active ministry convinced them that it was in himself.

The question of the degree to which withdrawal can be effected is one which appears to interest our contemporaries and to be a subject for discussion in both philosophical and scientific circles. Not many years ago in Germany the philosopher Edmund Husserl attacked one phase of the problem. If we are to get our meanings clear, he argued, we must go through a process of "bracketing" our conceptions, cutting them off from any connection not only with emotion but with the ordinary experiences we have in the world of time and space. To read Husserl is to feel that there is a sense in which ideas can and should be taken in isolation, abstracted from their surroundings, and either examined in the cold light of logic or admired for their formal beauty, according to the purposes we have for them. Husserl's great difficulty was in showing how the return from idea to active life is made. But the difficulty disappears when we refuse to restrict "reason" to one of its phases. What we actually find in life is a process of reasoning that employs first one, then another type of activity. The facts must be gathered, then compared; ideas may be enjoyed as ends, then exploited as means.

Examples of this kind of alternation are familiar in the mystical literature, as we have seen. It is interesting to find something not wholly unlike it beginning to appear in contemporary writing about science. We stand today in amazed terror before the towering mushroom-shaped body of scientific fact which threatens our destruction. Our emotion is half terror for ourselves and half amazement that the same science which once seemed morally so indifferent should reveal such breath-taking possibilities for good or evil. The fact seems to be that science is both remote and relevant and that our attitude must combine the detachment of the impartial worker with the passionate interest of the person whose life is at stake. As Professor Robert Oppenheimer has said, there is "a deep complementarity between its social justification and what is for the individual scientist his compelling motive in its pursuit." "In the past," says another distinguished research worker, "we scientists have gone into the laboratory to find truth. And as we entered we closed the door behind to shut out the world of man. Never again will we do that. If we are to find the truth that door must be left open."

Science's peculiar combination of dispassionateness and passion, of detachment on the one hand from practical and moral concerns and complete immersion in them on the other, becomes clear when we consider that it is both a body of neutral facts—useful either for good or evil—and also a method of inquiry with profoundly moral implications. Indeed, if we are looking for an example of loyalty to moral standards we need go no farther than the scientific method itself. In the first place, where do we find a more striking object lesson of the immorality of wishful thinking? "Be sure your sin will find you out," especially if it is the sin of dishonesty, might well be inscribed over every laboratory door. In the second place, where is there a more dramatic instance of the triumph of co-operation? Science cannot tolerate disagreement and insists on overcoming it. The obligation to follow the golden rule, to put oneself in another's place and to rule out private prejudice, is paramount. Third, where can we look for a better illustration of the religious experience of devotion to an end in itself than in the attitude of the truly devoted scientist who, in Huxley's words, "sits down before fact as a little child"? For special purposes of its own, science knows how to withdraw to the area where disinterestedness and impartiality reign. But the door is kept open. The connection with the moral problem is never obscured.

We have spoken of the problem of return and have tried to illustrate the difficulty a rational faith has in facing practical problems by pointing to the similar difficulties confronting our institutions of learning. Before closing these lectures let us go back to our original example of a group of college students who are concerned with the religious life and ask whether the experience of such a group of students in our own time has any light to throw on our problem. It seems to me that the more one considers the work of the college Christian Association the more one finds in it the kind of help in effecting return that a rational faith needs. The great dilemma of college life arises from the dubious fact that we seem to serve two masters. As students we must be open-minded, impartial, balanced in our judgments, always waiting for new evidence.

But as persons we have definite convictions about God and his will for us. Should we not admit the dilemma? The living truth is that we are both free and bound—free to inquire and bound to certain loyalties. Why, then, should not our work in the classroom represent one type of interest, and that in the religious association another? What is involved, after all, is not the pressure of two opposing forces but an alternation of interest such as withdrawal and return. There is a time for weighing evidence and another for acting on such evidence as we have. The balance is delicate but the lives of the most gifted human beings show us that in the forward thrust of personal experience a dynamic synthesis can be achieved. There is no difficulty about serving two masters if their names are God and Truth.

A religious group in college can help, therefore, to supplement the bookish one-sidedness into which the life of reason is apt to drift by reminding its members of the practical decisions that are part of Christian experience. It can keep the immediate moral issue vividly before the student's mind. It can bring him the support of his fellows in his own and other institutions. Above all, it can testify constantly that his religious purposes are his own and are not forced on him by any outside authority. We should not be too much disturbed if the numbers affected are small. Actually the group of students able to absorb the best in college life has always been limited. As a matter of record, has not the truth often been entrusted to a saving minority? The odds against the remnant that remains should remind us simply that we live in a temporal world where God's purposes are often thwarted and where no triumph of the spirit can be complete. In the light of the terrifying problems we face today this fact takes on added meaning. Although we may not expect to have all our questions answered we are bound to answer as many as we can. In spite of our difficulties we are blind indeed if we do not see that some good ends are being accomplished and that the effort to align ourselves with the forces at work in their behalf is worth while. War is here but so is the fight against it. The problems of industry and race are very much with us but our students are alert to their meaning and equipped to deal with them as never before. Theological and moral doubts are widely prevalent but the opportunities to know the truth about ourselves, our world, and the aims of our common life were never more rich.

The religious losses with which we began our study may not be allowed, then, to have the last word. Faith, grounded in the buoyant affirmations of life, refuses to be downed. But faith, in college as elsewhere, cannot use the formulas of a world we have left behind. The neo-orthodox seem not to see how alien that world was and for this reason we were forced to disagree with them. Yet we accepted their stress on the need for practical action. In our effort to recover for ourselves some of the moral decisiveness they so admirably exemplify we suggested that even in our academic life the tragic facts of suffering might be given a more prominent place. Suffering is the central experience of life. The mysteriousness of its extent and its distribution poses our darkest problems. But the answers, so far as they are found, lead not back toward authority but forward into a productive union of sensitive feeling, consistent thought, and remedial work. In the Biblical tradition itself we found support for the view that the will of God works not arbitrarily but through man's own gropings for the deeper truths of emotion and reason. Exploring the task of the college we discovered that both the aesthetic and the intellectual tasks set us make clear the profounder rhythms of withdrawal and return which religion, with its need for both contemplation and action, brings most sharply into relief. Throughout it has been obvious that withdrawal is easier than return and that a rational faith must be particularly careful to seek out the deeper ranges of emotional sensitiveness on the one hand and the responsibilities of decision and action on the other.

A final illustration from architecture may help us to see both how incomplete idea is when cut off from life and life is when separated from idea, and also how naturally and easily in faith based on reason they can combine. Let us imagine ourselves standing in turn in front of three famous buildings. The first represents withdrawal to the world of pure form. The second emphasizes life and motion but without benefit of idea. The third brings idea and feeling together in a harmonious and satisfying equilibrium.

The first of these buildings is the Taj Mahal. Most people who have seen it agree that it is one of the most beautiful in the world. As you view it across a pool of water lined with cypress trees and feel the perfect symmetry of dome and minaret you have an impression of absolute perfection. Even the glare of the white marble has been relieved by writing the entire Koran in inlay work of precious stones. "This is finality," you exclaim. The last word has been spoken, the last stroke of the architect's pencil drawn, and nothing remains to be added.

If you couple with this the experience of observing Moslem worshipers in the Friday service at a mosque your impression of finality is confirmed but in a different sense. As you watch long rows of men going through the ritual with complete uniformity in their bowing, kneeling, and rising, you feel the finality of the military drill for which also the last word has been spoken. The Moslem in making the great surrender of Islam has given up individuality just as the soldier must, to identify himself with a cause. The muezzin calling to prayer from the minaret is a sentinel calling to arms. To obey the call means to join an army of worshipers for whom the command is laid down in the form of revelation. In this case, however, the Word has become not flesh but stone. It has been spoken once and for all, the tradition has crystallized, and any chance for growth or for adaptation to the changing needs of men has been cut off.

In South India, at Hindu Madura, you can have a very different experience. There the great gopuras or towers of the temple of Menakshi rise above the city, each tower covered with hundreds of statues of gods, each god provided not with two but with half a dozen arms and a similar number of legs. The interior of the temple shows none of the order and symmetry of the Taj Mahal but a bewildering confusion of corridors and passages. It sprawls over acres of ground without apparent plan and resembles the Hindu philosophy itself where beliefs of every sort have been admitted without clear definition or the appeal to consistency. The Hindu temple and philosophy both make one think of the jungle, where growth is quick and uncontrolled, with a feverish development and equally speedy decay. The pruning knife of the gardener and that of the logician have been kept away. This, you say to yourself, is not finality but fecundity and fertility where form is at a discount and impulse, desire, and wayward purpose mark the upward thrust of life.

I am not using these illustrations to belittle creeds that are different from ours. At a time like the present when the idea of a United Nations is struggling to be born and when there is less excuse than ever before for failing to see the good in other traditions it ill becomes us to point the finger of scorn at anyone but ourselves. My point is simply that these buildings stand for habits of mind that are operative the world over. Even on our own college campuses we find men and women who worship at the Taj Mahal. An instance is the college student who says: My father's religion (or politics or economic point of view) is good enough for me and I need go no further. These are the traditionalists who refuse to fit their views to an experimental age. Standing with them are the idealists in an abstract sense for whom the idea retains its purity only when it is untouched by the press of human events. Both worship abstract names and both need to be reminded that the Taj Mahal, which stands for tradition and for harmony, is itself a tomb.

On the other hand, our colleges contain many worshipers at the Hindu temple of Menakshi. They are the thoughtless ones for whom each passing desire of the moment is of supreme importance. Included also are the less selfish and more high-minded group who are so immersed in the practical task that the college's opportunity for reflection on ideas as well as sheer enjoyment of the beautiful makes little appeal.

Need I press the point that each has a partial view and that the demands of both can be satisfied? An illustration which combines the two is the mosque of Hagia Sophia at Istanbul. As you stand under its great central dome with the half-domes on either side and see the corridors stretching out into remote distances it seems as if you were at the center of the universe and as if the world reached out infinitely in every direction. Here, you feel, is not finality nor fecundity but the limitless potentiality of the human soul as it faces the possibility for spiritual growth under guidance from above. For the most impressive part of the whole scene is the light which streams in through the windows of the cupola bringing with it both illumination and pattern. The ends of the corridors remain invisible. The question of where life came from and whither it tends, is still shrouded in mystery. But the eagerness and challenge of the present moment are given direction by the light from above which dominates the scene.

In its presence how futile seems much of our talk about whether this higher light should be called revelation or reason. The mosque itself, built originally by Justinian as a Christian church, was named Hagia Sophia, Sacred Wisdom, as if to suggest that wisdom, coming from above and imposing its will upon our wayward natural desires, must always have the force of revelation since it means a break with the life of impulse. At the same time revelation can only speak reasonably to us with the voice of wisdom since God, whatever else he may be, is the God of truth. So far as architecture can take on the appearance of life this building gives us a feeling of tension, with its cupola supported by pendentives, its interplay of light and darkness, and its over-all suggestion of the world outside that beckons to the life within. But the tension is resolved as the light from the cupola pushes the darkness back and as the worshiper realizes that mystery and pain can progressively be overcome through the influence of the wisdom which comes from on high. Mind and heart can join in a faith which holds that God is first of all a God of truth and that what leads to truth must lead to God himself.

Index